The
Covenant
Meal

The Covenant Meal

David Matthew

Harvestime

**Published in the United Kingdom by:
Harvestime Services Ltd, 136 Hall Lane, Bradford,
West Yorkshire BD4 7DG**

Copyright © 1988 David Matthew
First published by Harvestime
First printed March 1988

Scripture quotations are generally taken from the New
International Version. Copyright © 1978 by the New
York International Bible Society and published by
Hodder & Stoughton. Used by permission.

British Library Cataloguing in Publication Data

Matthew, David
  The covenant meal
  1. Title
  264'.36

  ISBN 0-947714-51-0

Typeset by: Ocean Typesetting,
St. Michael's Hall, Bennett Road,
Headingley, Leeds LS6 3HN, West Yorkshire
Printed and bound in the United Kingdom by: Richard
Clay Ltd, Bungay, Suffolk

Contents

To Peter
'A wise son brings joy to his father'
(Proverbs 10:1)

1

Rite of confusion

In a Spanish cathedral I once sat in on a Roman Catholic mass. Incense filled the air, adding to the atmosphere of solemnity and mystery created by the lavish decorations behind the altar, the candles, the embroidered vestments of the priest, the throb of the mighty organ that accompanied the chants, and the pillars soaring into the gloom of the vaulted roof.

The sense of awe reached its peak as the priest pronounced the words of consecration, 'This is my body', and held aloft the host for worship.

By contrast, as a young man I often attended holy communion at a 'low' Anglican church. The form was simple and the people's sincerity beyond doubt, even if the service did progress 'by the book'. The invitation to 'feed on Christ in your heart by faith' found a ready response in my spirit, and I always went away blessed.

More often, though, I 'remembered the Lord' among the Open Brethren. From childhood I became used to the Sunday morning 'breaking of bread', where hymns from *The Believers Hymn Book* focused our attention on the sufferings of Christ on our behalf. Preaching or testimony before the taking of the bread and wine would have been unthinkable, a distraction from our primary interest — the cross of our Lord.

As I chewed on the bread, which passed from hand to hand

in absolute silence, I would screw up my eyes in an effort to 'see' Jesus hanging on the cross for me. I pictured, as I had been taught to do, the crown of thorns, the nails, the wounds, the blood.

Again, I recall a conversation in a university hall of residence:

'We couldn't take communion this morning,' complained one student. 'The vicar was preaching somewhere else and the curate, who was supposed to officiate, didn't turn up. So we had to do without.'

'Why couldn't someone else do it?' queried one of the others, a Pentecostal.

'Because there was no other ordained person present.'

'What's that got to do with it?'

'Everything, of course! Only an ordained person can officiate at holy communion. I thought everybody knew that.'

'Show me chapter and verse for it, then.'

'Well, I don't know about that, but . . . .'

And so the exchange continued, long into the evening, generating more heat than light.

Cassava and cold tea

In central Africa I joined a group of worshippers in partaking of cassava mush and cold tea laced with vinegar, obeying Christ's command, 'Do this in remembrance of me,' in the middle of the bush, miles from anywhere.

Back in England, I once shared bread and wine with a boisterous bunch of God's people in a house, with much mingling, greeting of each other, prayer and laughter. One cheerful soul at my elbow shouted across the room, 'Hey, Pete, throw us a bit of bread over, will you?'

Pete obliged. The piece of bread sailed over the heads of the crowd to a neat catch and consumption by two young men whose sincerity and love for the Lord were beyond question. A far cry from the solemn ritual of the cathedral!

I have attended meetings of the Salvation Army and the Quakers who, as a matter of policy, never take communion at all.

Elsewhere, I have eaten wafers both round and square, bread leavened and unleavened, torn apart by hand or neatly cubed beforehand, bread brown and white, sliced and unsliced, fresh and stale. I have drunk wine from silver chalices, earthenware mugs, individual thimble-sized glasses and plain glass tumblers, containing wine both fermented and unfermented.

At one chapel the steward discovered just before the service that the wine had run out. No shops being open, he rushed across the road to the house of one of the members, who provided half a jar of raspberry jam. Mixed with water and stirred vigorously, it passed for wine, even if the seeds did get stuck in our teeth.

Some celebrate the Lord's Supper daily. Others maintain there is a biblical case for weekly celebration - and that it must be on the first day of the week, the Lord's day. Oddly, they would usually insist that the supper be eaten in the morning! Others again make it a monthly ritual tagged on to the end of a normal Sunday service, or even an annual one, celebrated preferably at Eastertide.

The nature of the act is as disputed as its frequency. Those who regard it as a mere memorial of Christ's death express horror at the Roman Catholic and 'high church' conviction that it repeats the sacrifice of Christ, whose body and blood are offered again to God upon the altar by a priest. And vice versa. A whole range of intermediate views lie between the two.

Knock-on effect

The doctrine of the Lord's Supper does not stand in isolation. It has a way of touching a whole range of Christian attitudes. Recently, for example, it has been at the centre of the debate on the ordination of women. With regard to that debate, the Bishop of Salisbury shrewdly observed, 'Some of the important issues are not specifically about the role of women at all, but about the eucharist.'[1]

The main argument here revolves around the 'iconic' view of the ministry. On this view, the person presiding at communion is seen as an 'icon' (image) of Christ as he presided at the Last Supper. He should, therefore, be an image of Christ in his maleness. A woman cannot truly represent the *man* Christ Jesus.

This approach makes some major assumptions, notably that the presiding person must be a member of the clergy, that is, a body of men fitted by ordination to perform certain holy functions forbidden to the laity. It assumes also that he is a priest representing Christ.

Vast numbers of sincere Christians, however, would dissent from such a view, arguing for the priesthood of all believers and the right of *any* sincere Christian to break the bread and dispense the wine. To them, the arguments about women's ministry revolve around different issues altogether.

Legitimate questions

If the charismatic renewal, with its temporary breaking down of denominational barriers, has performed any service to the body of Christ, it must include its fostering of a new awareness of the variety in Christian practice. More of God's people now refuse to accept without question the traditional practices of their denominations. Increasingly they are asking, 'Why . . . ?'

How, may I ask, do *you* view the Lord's Supper? Do you understand what you are doing as you partake of it? What thoughts run through your mind as you eat and drink?

How often do you celebrate it? Annually? Monthly? Weekly? Daily? Periodically? What governs your choice?

Have you ever questioned your denomination's practice? Do you regard the Lord's Supper as a duty or a pleasure? What, if anything, do you expect to gain from participating?

Questions like these force us to face the matter of authority in spiritual things. I must put my cards on the table here and state my conviction that the only legitimate authority is the Bible. Once tradition (even allegedly Spirit-led tradition) is allowed to intrude, chaos is guaranteed. Church history is the proof of it. It is to the touchstone of Scripture, therefore, that we must bring the confused issue of the Lord's Supper.

It is my conviction also that the Holy Spirit is active in restoration. In every generation he draws to the attention of God's people certain truths and emphases which, though present in Scripture from the beginning, have long been ignored or overlooked. The title of this book — *The Covenant Meal* — points to the emphasis regarding the Lord's Supper which I believe the Spirit of God to be restoring today.

The laying aside of preconceptions is no easy task. Some would say it is impossible. But let's at least attempt it as we look into Scripture for light on this vital topic. And let our searching be done, not out of academic interest, but with a mind to be 'doers of the word'. Only doers are blessed.

Chapter 1 NOTES

1. Quoted in C. Howard, *The Ordination of Women to the Priesthood*, CIO Publishing, 1984, p57

2

Roots in the Passover

The *Lord's* Supper began with the *Last* Supper. And the Last Supper was a Passover meal.

We call it the Last Supper, of course, because it was the final meal shared by Jesus and his inner circle of followers before his crucifixion. The Bible records the event in Matthew 26, Mark 14, Luke 22 and 1 Corinthians 11. It took place, in fact, on the very night of his arrest, when he made his way to an upper room 'to eat the Passover' with his disciples (Luke 22:8).

And what exactly was the Passover? Without an understanding of it we cannot appreciate what it means to take the bread and wine of communion. So let's remind ourselves of this important Old Testament event.

Of all the great feasts of Israel, the Passover was the greatest — and the oldest. It was the annual celebration of that turning point in Israel's history when, after four centuries under the slavemaster's whip in Egypt, God miraculously brought the people out and pointed them towards the promised land where they were to live as a free nation under his rule.

It was a festival of deliverance from slavery and of a new beginning. And for us Christians it is a vivid picture of our own deliverance from a spiritual Egypt of slavery to sin and of our new beginning in Christ.

The great deliverance

Exodus 12 records the story. Moses, you will recall, had
graduated from God's school in the desert of Midian after
his forty-year course. He emerged with no degrees or diplomas
but with a much-mellowed character. The hotheaded prince
of Egypt had become a man of God and now, equipped with
miraculous powers and God's own words, he arrived in Egypt
with a tall order for a proud Pharaoh: 'This is what the Lord,
the God of Israel, says: "Let my people go."'

Far from rushing to obey, Pharaoh dug in his heels — just
as Satan does today in his reluctance to see his slaves released
into the hands of a merciful God. At Moses' word, therefore,
God brought a succession of nine awful plagues upon the
Egyptians, each one designed to show the superiority of the
living God of Israel over the pagan deities of Egypt (Exodus
7 — 11).

It was a fearful time. The rivers turned to blood. Frogs,
gnats and flies hopped and buzzed till the Egyptians were
driven mad. The livestock succumbed to a fatal disease, then
the few animals that remained — and the people themselves
— broke out in boils. In the wake of freak hailstorms that
crushed the standing crops came swarms of locusts to strip
the country of its greenery. Finally, God blotted out the sun
to plunge Egypt into a three-day spell of near-tangible
darkness.

Still Pharaoh remained unyielding. But even the proudest
enemy of God (and none is prouder than Satan) has his
breaking point, and Pharaoh's came with the tenth plague:
the death of the firstborn of every Egyptian family, 'from
the firstborn son of Pharaoh, who sits on the throne, to the
firstborn son of the slave girl, who is at her hand mill, and
all the firstborn of the cattle as well'.

Preparations

In readiness for the great packing of bags and moving out
which this plague would prompt, the Israelites were to make

certain preparations. Each family was instructed to take a year-old male lamb and observe it for a time to check that it was free from defect — a wonderful picture of the sinless life of our Lord Jesus, God's perfect Lamb.

Then they were to slaughter the animal and paint some of its blood on to the sides and tops of the door-frames of their houses. Born-again believers get excited as they read this. What a powerful picture it presents of the blood of Christ shed on the cross and applied to their own lives and that of their fellow-believers!

God commanded a *meal*, too. What a marvellously practical God he is: he didn't want them trekking into the unknown on an empty stomach! Within their blood-marked houses they were to dine on roast lamb, along with bitter herbs and unleavened bread (that is, made without yeast). They were to feast on the very lamb whose shed blood was the price of their deliverance, just as we, who are the beneficiaries of Christ's shed blood, now feed on him by faith. The one Lamb provides both salvation and sustenance.

This Passover meal was to be no leisurely affair, however. They were to risk indigestion by eating it in haste, with staff in hand, cloaks tucked into belts and sandals on, ready for the 'off' which was to sound as soon as the dire truth of the death of the firstborn dawned upon the plague-weary Egyptians.

'On that night,' promised the Lord, 'I will pass through Egypt and strike down every firstborn — both men and animals — and I will bring judgment on all the gods of Egypt; I am the Lord. The blood will be a sign for you on the houses where you are; and when I see the blood, I will *pass over* you. No destructive plague will touch you when I strike Egypt.'

And that's exactly how it happened. 'At midnight the Lord struck down all the firstborn in Egypt . . . and there was loud wailing in Egypt, for there was not a house without someone dead.'

Pharaoh at last changed his tune, urging the Israelites to

hurry and get out of the country, adding a pathetic 'And also bless me.' Thus began one of the greatest mass migrations in human history. It was The Exodus, the great moving-out.

Feast of remembrance

Such a great event merited remembrance. The Israelites' future as a free nation, God insisted, must always be remembered as hinging upon this mighty deliverance. To fix it in their memory, God instituted the Passover feast. It was to be Israel's annual celebration of his saving power and the meal which proclaimed his faithfulness as a covenant-keeping God.

Held in the month of Nisan (March-April), the celebration of the feast, like the original Passover, was to revolve round the eating of roast lamb with bitter herbs and unleavened bread.

Each item was calculated to trigger memories. The lamb was of double significance. It illustrated the principle of *substitution:* a lamb had died instead of the Israelite firstborn — just as a ram had earlier gone to the altar in place of the patriarch Isaac, and just as Jesus, God's ultimate Lamb, would die, 'the righteous for the unrighteous' to bring us to God (1 Peter 3:18).

The lamb was also a token of *God's concern for their physical welfare* — that they should not be hungry as they began their journey through the desert. It's good to remember that he is still concerned for the physical (as well as for the spiritual, mental and emotional) welfare of his people. Unlike many Christians today, God doesn't carve us up into spirit, soul and body, emphasising the first two at the expense of the third; he cares for us *as whole people*. And, as we shall see, our eating of the Lord's Supper, the Christian equivalent of the Passover, has implications of a highly physical nature (1 Corinthians 11:28-30).

The bitter herbs recalled the *bunches of hyssop* the Israelites had used as brushes for painting that vital blood on their door-posts. And even more telling, perhaps: the face-creasing bitterness they experienced as the herbs touched their taste-buds acted as a keen reminder of the *bitterness of the long slavery* from which the shed blood had rescued them.

The unleavened bread brought to mind the *haste* with which they had left Egypt, haste which had prevented their waiting for yeasted bread to rise before baking and eating it. Urged out of the land by Pharaoh, 'the people took their dough before the yeast was added, and carried it on their shoulders in kneading troughs wrapped in clothing'.

But it was more than that. In Hebrew thinking, yeast or leaven soon became a common symbol of *corruption*. In this respect, the eating of unleavened bread at the Passover feast would remind them that, by the events of the original Passover, they had not only been separated *from* the evils of Egypt but also separated *to* a holy God. Leaving sin behind, they were to be holy, just as God himself was holy. And the same applies to us (Leviticus 11:44-45; 1 Peter 1:15-16)!

The celebratory eating of bread without yeast went on, in fact, for a whole week each year, immediately following the Passover feast. It was the Festival of Unleavened Bread, a picture of the holiness of life to which we are called today as God's New Testament people. As Paul was to point out many centuries later, we Christians are to 'keep the Festival, not with the old yeast, the yeast of malice and wickedness, but with bread without yeast, the bread of sincerity and truth' (1 Corinthians 5:8).

The Passover, God said, was to be 'a lasting ordinance', one to endure throughout future generations. True to his command, generation after generation of Jews kept the feast until, some thirteen centuries after its institution, we find Jesus and his disciples celebrating the Passover in that upper room, at the Last Supper.

But change was imminent. On God's calendar, the ministry of Jesus marked the ending of one era and the beginning of a new one. Events were about to take place at Calvary and the garden tomb which would completely overshadow even the great exodus from Egypt. Because those events would mark a radical change in God's dealings with his people, they would also require a radical change in the feast his people observed.

During the Last Supper, therefore, Jesus made a startling move: he broke into the long-established Passover routines and gave them a completely new direction! He ordered the Passover feast off stage to make room for — the Lord's Supper.

A better feast

Jews still keep the Passover today, and to be present at its celebration is a deeply moving experience. Family life, faith and a sense of racial identity receive an annual underlining which can only be beneficial.

But how sad that, in failing to recognise Jesus as their Messiah, the Jews also fail to see God's far *greater* provision for family life, for faith and for a national identity which transcends Jewishness. This is the new international, non-racial 'holy nation' (1 Peter 2:9) in which barriers of race, colour, pedigree and social class come tumbling down and where 'Christ is all, and is in all' (Colossians 3:11) — the church!

What a joy and privilege to belong to this new nation! We look back to a more oppressive slavery than that of Egypt, from which we have been delivered by the death of a better lamb — the spotless Lamb of God. Our new nationhood — and hence our new sense of security and identity — is rooted in God himself and, like him, is eternal, good for both this life and the one to come.

In the meantime we celebrate a feast, a festival of deliverance and rejoicing called the Lord's Supper. While, as we have seen, it has its roots in the Passover, it surpasses the Jewish feast in every way. Let's now consider how Jesus brought it into being.

3

Passover redefined

What exactly did Jesus do to change the time-honoured Jewish Passover?

Over the centuries since its inauguration, the annual celebration had gradually settled into a regular procedure. It would be helpful as this stage to understand that procedure, so let's briefly run through it.

When the family and friends had assembled, the meal would begin with the first of four cups of red wine — the *cup of consecration* — and the ritual handwashing of the man (usually the head of the family) who was to preside over the meal.

Lettuce or parsley was then eaten, dipped first in salt water. It stood for the hyssop used by their ancestors to paint the lamb's blood on to their doorframes. The salt water represented the bitter tears caused by their slavery in Egypt and also the waters of the Red Sea through which God later brought them in triumph — their 'baptism into one body'.

Next came the first breaking of unleavened bread, symbolic of the 'bread of affliction' eaten in Egypt. At this point, the president would outline, in answer to the question, 'What does this ceremony mean to you?' (Exodus 12:26; 13:8), the events from Abraham to Moses which gave the Passover meal its significance. It was a proclamation of the goodness of God.

Then, after the singing of Psalms 113 and 114, the second

cup was filled and handed to the president, who would drink and pass it to the others. Because it followed on from the president's proclaiming of God's dealings with the people of Israel, this was called the *cup of proclamation*.

At this point everybody present washed their hands and grace was said. Then some bitter herbs were placed between pieces of bread, dipped in a paste and eaten. The paste, known as *charosheth*, symbolised the clay with which the Hebrew slaves had been forced to make bricks in Egypt. It was made of dates, apples, pomegranates and nuts, and had cinnamon sticks running through it, symbolising the straw used to bind the clay together.

You will remember that Pharaoh's refusal to set the slaves free had gone hand in hand with the imposing upon them of an extra burden: they had now been forced to find their own straw. To a people already crushed by hard labour this had been well nigh unbearable — the last straw, we might say! It was the final setback before deliverance came, and thus worthy of specific remembrance at the Passover feast.

A piece of bread dipped in the paste was sometimes known as a sop, and it seems likely that this is what Jesus gave to Judas at the Last Supper (John 13:26).

The meal proper

Up to this point in the Passover, the eating was symbolic only, the guests taking only very small pieces. Its purpose was to awaken memory. But now the meal took a different turn: the satisfying of hunger. The people ate in earnest, for the roast lamb had to be consumed in its entirety, any leftovers being burnt. There would be much laughter and merriment as formality gave way to the relaxed enjoyment of a good dinner.

The meal finished with the washing of hands, the eating up of any remaining Passover bread and a long thanksgiving for the food consumed.

Then came the third cup, the *cup of thanksgiving*, which was drunk with the short prayer: 'Blessed are you, O Lord our God, King of the universe, who have created the fruit of the vine.' Remember this cup, because it is the one that Jesus was to invest with new significance.

Psalms 115 to 118 and Psalm 136 were sung next, followed by the drinking of the *fourth and last cup*. Then, with more prayers, a shout and a final prayer of praise to God, the Passover celebration would come to an end.

This, then, was the kind of well-rehearsed routine that the disciples of Jesus expected to follow as they climbed the stairs to the upper room on that fateful evening. After all, they had done it every year of their lives. Little did they know, as they reclined at table with Jesus, that events were to take an altogether different turn.

A radical turnaround

To begin with, the meal seems to have progressed in the normal way. Luke, in his account of the Last Supper, mentions two cups. The first of these was in all likelihood the second one in the Passover ritual. That, you will remember, was the *cup of proclamation*, which was filled and handed first to the president of the feast — in this case Jesus (Luke 22:17).

Shortly afterwards, as the symbolic part of the meal continued, Jesus handed the sop to Judas, who promptly departed, leaving the rest of the company to enjoy the meal proper. The hungry disciples no doubt tucked into the roast lamb with enthusiasm, grateful that, in the down-to-earth way of the God of Israel, he had ordained that the symbolic should merge with the gastronomic!

You will recall that once the roast lamb had been eaten, everybody would wash their hands and *eat up any Passover bread which remained*. This was a kind of natural lull in the celebration, a pause to tidy up before the next stage. And it was at this point, it seems, marked by the words 'He took bread', that Jesus gave a new direction to the proceedings. A minor part of the routine — finishing off the bread — was elevated by Jesus to new importance.

In the phrase 'He *took* bread' (Luke 22:19), 'took' is an active word suggesting initiative. It is a different word altogether from the one used in verse 17 — 'After *taking* the cup . . .' — which means no more than a passive receiving according to the Passover custom.

In short, the familiar routine, which in a sense almost ran itself, driven by its own historical momentum, was being overridden. Jesus was now taking over. In a divine initiative, 'He took bread, gave thanks and broke it, and gave it to them, saying, "This is my body given for you; do this in remembrance of *me.*"'

What an astonishing and radical turnabout! This had never been part of the Passover procedure. If routine takes away the need to think and calculate, a break in routine has the very opposite effect, and the disciples' minds were suddenly jolted into action. What exactly was Jesus saying?

As their understanding hurried to catch up with the situation, gradually it began to dawn upon them what a profound change he was proposing: their remembrance was no longer to be of God's deliverance from the slavery of Egypt, but *of Jesus himself!*

Could it be that Jesus, this friend of theirs, was *so* important? True, they called him Lord and Master, but was he of such significance in God's great scheme of things that he outshone in importance even Moses and the deliverance from Egypt? And what right had any man to override the hallowed ritual of the Passover? Yet Jesus had done so confidently and without apology!

While their minds continued to grapple with these momentous issues, Jesus was breaking more new ground. In a further initiative, 'after the supper he took the cup' (v20).

This was the third of the Passover cups. Coming just 'after the supper' — the main, hunger-satisfying part of the meal — it was *the cup of thanksgiving*. It is to this cup that Paul later refers when he says, 'Is not the cup of thanksgiving for which we give thanks a participation in the blood of Christ?' (1 Corinthians 10:16).

Jesus now held that cup in his hands. 'This cup,' he declared to the astonished disciples, 'is the new covenant in my blood, which is poured out for you.'

Again, he was setting a whole new direction, drawing attention away from the events of the old covenant and the blood of a lamb and focusing instead on the *new* covenant and on '*my* blood'. (We shall see in another chapter the significance of the covenant reference.)

The disciples must have been stunned. Who *was* this Jesus who could claim such importance for himself? They thought they knew him, but perhaps they didn't after all (that's probably true of *us*, too).

Conflicting ideas from recent times churned around in their minds. Nathanael's 'Can anything good come out of Nazareth?' vied with Jesus' implicit claim to deity in assuring the paralytic, 'Your sins are forgiven.' The 'prophet without honour in his own country', they remembered, was the one who had shone with divine radiance on the Mount of Transfiguration.

And now this. Jesus, their friend, reclining there at the crumb-covered, gravy-spotted table in all his apparent normality, was coolly making claims for himself which boggled their minds!

Did Jesus and his disciples, I wonder, go on to finish the traditional Passover proceedings? It seems unlikely. The pattern had been for ever broken. Jesus, the radical, had taken the whole time-honoured affair and turned it right around. Now, with the imminent sacrifice of himself as the Lamb of God who fulfilled all that the Passover lambs had ever symbolised (1 Corinthians 5:7), the Passover was declared redundant and the Lord's Supper inaugurated in its place.

He had selected two of the Passover's key elements — bread and wine — and given them a whole new meaning connected with his own person. The rest could safely be discarded. Who wants to hang on to the oyster once he has extracted the pearl?

4

Meals:
more than food

The Lord's Supper is a meal. A symbolic meal, perhaps, but a meal nonetheless: we eat bread and drink wine in the same way as we might eat toast and drink coffee at breakfast. In trying to get to the roots of the Lord's Supper, therefore, it might be a good idea to start with meals in general.

What exactly *is* a meal? In its most basic form, I suppose, it is the satisfying of hunger and thirst by placing food and drink into the mouth and swallowing them. But that's a bit *too* basic, like describing a violin solo as horse-hair rubbed across stretched gut!

There's much more to a meal than swallowing food and drink. It's a time for *togetherness*. 'Come round for a meal,' we say, meaning, 'Spend an evening with us, talking, laughing and enjoying friendship around the table.' The social element is vital.

And if pushing food and drink down our throats is all there is to it, why do we so often spread a nice tablecloth, lay out the cutlery neatly, put flowers on the table and serve up the lovingly-prepared food on our best dinner-plates, with tureens and gravy-boat to match? It's because a meal is an *occasion*, a carefully planned focus of effort corresponding to the value we place upon our friendship with the guests.

A businessmen will strike a deal over a meal at an expensive restaurant, implicitly saying to the other party, 'I consider you and what you have to offer worth the courtesy and expense of this lavish luncheon.' Outstanding events like birthdays, weddings and anniversaries are marked by meals. And would Christmas be the same without Christmas dinner?

Meals in Bible times

If a meal is more than food and drink today, it was all the more so in Bible times.

As well as having all the social implications just mentioned, a meal in those days often had religious ones, too, and was seen as a *sacred act uniting the eaters.*

Life, it was argued, was a gift of God, and food was the means he had provided for sustaining it. Eating, therefore, established sacred ties between dinner companions as well as between them and God. As P.T. Forsyth has put it, 'To eat the same food was to renew the blood from the same source; it was therefore the same blood.'[1]

In Jewish life around the time of Jesus, both the Qumran community and the Essenes — strict religious sects within Judaism — gave meals a high place in their scale of values. Only those initiated into the sect could participate, and every meal taken together was seen as a renewal of their corporate vows.

On the secular front, wedding feasts and funeral meals bound the partakers together. In Greek and Roman life, societies, guilds and trading groups had their common meals, which were for 'insiders' only. Worshippers of pagan deities would hold social gatherings in the temple of their particular god, declaring thereby their common allegiance. The Mystery Religions of the period also set great store by their religious meals.

Jesus was a guest at many meals. He dined at the family table of his friends Lazarus, Mary and Martha (Luke 10:38-42). He attended the wedding feast at Cana (John 2:1-11). He accepted the invitation of a Pharisee (Luke 7:36-50). In eating with them he extended his friendship towards them. He was saying, in effect, 'I'm happy to be associated with you.'

That's why the religious bigots of the day, who wouldn't have been seen dead at a 'sinner's' table, could never weigh Jesus up. It was his having dinner with tax collector Matthew that provoked their question to the disciples: 'Why does your teacher eat with tax collectors and "sinners"?' (Matthew 9:10-11). In their view — the universal view of the day — to eat with them was to associate with them. And that, of course, was exactly what Jesus wanted to do, in order to reach those needy people with his love and truth!

Meals and covenants

We have already seen that Israel's greatest festival was celebrated annually by a meal — the Passover — and that this was a token of the Lord's faithfulness to them as a covenant-keeping God. Here we must latch on to that word 'covenant', for it has a strong bearing on our understanding of meals generally in Bible times, and of the Lord's Supper in particular.

At that momentous meal, Jesus had offered the wine-cup to his disciples with the words, 'This cup is the new covenant in my blood.' His reference to a *new* covenant implied the existence of an *old* covenant which the new one was about to replace. Since covenant is referred to in all four accounts of the institution of the Lord's Supper, it is clearly an important concept. But what exactly *is* a covenant? And what is its connection with meals?

A covenant is a *solemn, binding agreement* between two parties. In the ancient Near East the practice was widespread, and the Old Testament offers numerous examples.

Isaac and Abimelech made a covenant (Genesis 26:25-31), translated in the New International Version as 'treaty' or 'sworn agreement'. In this case it was an agreement between two men previously at loggerheads to keep out of each other's hair — to respect each other's rights and do each other no harm. And, as was usual, *the covenant was sealed in the sharing of a meal:* 'Isaac then made a feast for them, and they ate and drank.'

Jacob and Laban did something similar (Genesis 31:44-55) and, in token of their covenant, Jacob 'offered a sacrifice there in the hill country and invited his relatives to a meal'.

David and Abner also made a covenant, or compact, at a time of sensitive political readjustment (2 Samuel 3:17-21), and once again a meal sealed the agreement: 'When Abner, who had twenty men with him, came to David at Hebron, David prepared a feast for him and his men.'

Marriage, too, is a covenant, a serious mutual commitment between a man and a woman. In the prophet Malachi's day, God complained about the marital unfaithfulness in Judah, where it had become commonplace for a man to break faith with the wife of his youth by divorce. This happened, said the prophet, even 'though she is your partner, the wife of your *marriage covenant*' (Malachi 2:14). Marriage covenants, too, like other covenants, were followed by a meal which brought together not only the bride and groom but also their families.

Meals, then, are indeed more than food and drink. Even today they have far-reaching social significance, but in Bible days they meant even more. We have seen how they were an essential part of every covenant. Now we must consider how they relate to *the* covenant.

Chapter 4 NOTES

1. P.T. Forsyth, *The Church and the Sacraments,* Longmans, Green & Co., 1917, p243

5

The
covenant meal

Many of the great men in the Bible could be described as 'saviours' — men like Moses and Gideon, who 'saved' Israel from the hands of their enemies. But only one can be called *the* Saviour: Jesus.

In the same way, while the Bible mentions many covenants, its main focus is on *the* covenant — the special arrangement made by God in which he undertakes to be our God and bless us. This great covenant came in two parts, called the old covenant and new covenant, or sometimes the Old Testament and New Testament.

'Testaments?' you say. 'I thought those were the two divisions of the Bible?'

They are indeed, but they are called testaments for a reason. 'Testament', you see, is just another word for 'covenant', and the two parts of the Bible take their names from what they describe. The Old Testament — Genesis to Malachi — describes the old covenant, while the New Testament — Matthew to Revelation — describes the new covenant. Let's take a closer look at them both.

The first covenant

In Hebrews 9:1 the old covenant is called 'the *first* covenant', in contrast to the *second*, or new, covenant which came later. God expressed it in several stages. He made an agreement

with Noah, for example, promising never again to destroy
life on earth by means of a flood (Genesis 9:8-17).

To Abraham and his descendants he covenanted to give
the land of Canaan (Genesis 15). For an aged and childless
man like Abraham, with no natural prospect of any
descendants at all, this promise was almost unbelievable. So
God underlined the solemnity of it by a strange ceremony.
Abraham was to take a heifer, a goat and a ram, cut each
of them into two pieces and lay them out in two rows. Then
God did his bit: 'A smoking fire pot with a blazing torch
appeared and passed between the pieces.'

Here we see the significance of the expression 'to make
a covenant'. Literally, it is 'to *cut* a covenant'. When two
men made a covenant they would commonly cut up animals
and walk between the two pieces (for example, Jeremiah
34:18-20). By their action they were saying, 'If I don't abide
by the conditions of this agreement, may I likewise be cut
in half. And just as the blood of these creatures has been
shed, may mine also be shed if I fail to honour my promise.'

In Genesis 17 God expanded on his covenant with
Abraham, undertaking to be his God and the God of his
descendants. A whole nation was to come from Abraham,
God was saying, and his covenant would embrace that nation
as a whole — the people of Israel.

Covenant blood

The agreement was no wishy-washy affair. Built into it were
some clear-cut conditions.

On Abraham's side, the condition was total consecration
to the Lord. This was symbolised by the rite of circumcision,
in the act of which, inevitably, *blood was shed*. Indeed, as
we have begun to see, shed blood was a feature of every
covenant. As the foreskin was cut off, Abraham was
proclaiming, 'So may I and my descendants be cut off from
the benefits of God's promised blessing if we back down on
the agreement.' The blood flowed and sealed the deal.

Eventually that nation of descendants came into being —

but as slaves in Egypt. The Passover that eventually brought about their release was a covenant affair; in undertaking to bring them out of slavery and into the promised land, God was acting on his earlier promises. So now, in line with that agreement, God insisted that they follow his instructions to the letter. This they did. Blood was shed — the Passover lambs were killed — and out the people came.

Once they were clear of Egypt and more readily identifiable as a nation, the time arrived for God to renew his covenant with them more particularly. After all, if God and Israel were to get on together, there would have to be a clear understanding of what each party expected of the relationship.

This milestone in Israel's history is described in Exodus 19 to 24. 'If you will obey me fully and keep my covenant,' said the Lord, 'then out of all nations you will be my treasured possession. Although the whole earth is mine, you will be for me a kingdom of priests and a holy nation.'

Notice that this was a unilateral arrangement. Men can't thrash out a bargain with God in the same way as they can with each other. No, God was calling the shots and inviting Israel's agreement.

The astounding thing is that God wanted to bother with sinful human beings at all. As a holy God, he had no obligation to dirty his hands, so to speak, but the fact that he took the initiative to do so is a measure of his amazing grace. That grace continues to flow towards his creatures, and it is our privilege to experience it today in a way more deep and thrilling than Israel could ever know.

But back to Exodus. The *terms* of the covenant were next set out: the people were to keep the law which God now gave them through Moses. Beginning with the Ten Commandments in chapter 20, Moses spelled out the law to the people in detail, so that they could see exactly what they were committing themselves to.

A document for signing

The modern equivalent would be a scene in a solicitor's office, with someone about to enter into a legal agreement. The solicitor makes sure the person fully understands the details of the agreement before handing him the pen to add his signature. With that signature the agreement is in force. All its conditions, benefits and penalties are binding.

A covenant was made binding, not by a signature on a legal document but, as we have seen, by the shedding of blood. Thus, the people of Israel first agreed to the terms (summarised in Deuteronomy 28) of the legal document called 'the Book of the Covenant'. They did this by declaring to Moses, 'Everything the Lord has said we will do' (Exodus 24:7). Then blood was shed: Moses offered sacrifices to God.

Scripture records the solemn moment: 'Moses then took the blood, sprinkled it on the people and said, *"This is the blood of the covenant* that the Lord has made with you in accordance with all these words"' (Exodus 24:8).

As we would expect, a *covenant meal* set the seal upon the proceedings. Representatives of the people went up Mount Sinai 'and saw the God of Israel . . . . But God did not raise his hand against these leaders of the Israelites; they saw God, and they ate and drank' (Exodus 24:9-11). It was the annual Passover meal, however, which continued as the people's major reminder of God's covenant mercy.

Sometimes this old covenant has been called the *covenant of works,* because it depended on Israel's works — their obedience to God's law — for its success. But we would be wiser to see it as a covenant of grace. God, after all, had no obligation to those people. As we have observed, he and they were not equal parties who could thrash out an agreement to their mutual advantage.

Far from it. God's reaching out to them was one-sided. A holy God was stretching out his hand in sovereign mercy to sinful men. It was an act of pure grace!

Nevertheless, the old covenant did *operate* by means of works, and therein lay its weakness: Israel failed to keep the terms of the covenant. They broke the agreement and, inevitably, the bitter penalties of Deuteronomy 28 came upon them in full: confusion, defeat, disease, social chaos, deprivation, famine and, ultimately, exile and dispersion.

They may have continued to celebrate the Passover as the covenant meal, but without the obedience to match it, the meal became a mockery. It was like continuing to wear a wedding ring, the symbol of unending fidelity in marriage, while committing adultery. A celebration of God's past grace without a commitment to present obedience cannot lead to future blessing.

God's new arrangement

However, God wasn't finished yet! Just when rebellious Israel was about to be expelled from Canaan in fulfilment of the covenant's curse, he sounded a note of hope through the prophet Jeremiah: ' "The time is coming," declares the Lord, "when I will make a *new* covenant with the house of Israel and with the house of Judah." '

This looked hopeful! God went on to give some exciting details: ' "It will not be like the covenant I made with their forefathers when I took them by the hand to lead them out of Egypt, because they broke my covenant, though I was a husband to them," declares the Lord.

' "This is the covenant I will make with the house of Israel after that time," ' declares the Lord. "I will put my law in their minds and write it on their hearts. I will be their God, and they will be my people.

' "No longer will a man teach his neighbour, or a man his brother, saying, 'Know the Lord,' because they will all know me, from the least of them to the greatest," declares the Lord. "For I will forgive their wickedness and will remember their sins no more" ' (Jeremiah 31:31-34).

What a promise! It sounded like a better deal altogether than the old covenant. The weakness of the old covenant lay, not in God, but in his people, the pull of whose sinful nature made obedience impossible. But the time was coming when Paul would be able to write: 'What the law was powerless to do in that it was weakened by the sinful nature, God did by sending his own Son' (Romans 8:3).

Notice the words *'God* did'. His sovereign grace, which had reached to lost men in the old covenant, found even more lavish expression in the new one. By an act of grace in the person of his Son, God made it possible for men to be freed from the downward pull of a sinful nature and, instead, be able to 'participate in the *divine* nature and escape the corruption in the world caused by evil desires' (2 Peter 1:4).

What's the point in mopping up the water in my sitting-room if I don't first attend to the leak in the roof? It makes sense to deal with the cause before the effects. And that's exactly what God was saying he would do in the new covenant: he would change men's very nature so that they would be both able and willing to obey him!

This is what Jeremiah meant when he spoke about God's law being written on the people's minds and hearts. Instead of inscribing his law on tablets of stone, an outward ideal towards which they strove in vain, God would inscribe it inwardly. He would make God-pleasing the mainspring, the driving force, of their very being.

This was something to look forward to indeed. What a great new covenant! What an amazingly wonderful divine arrangement!

Now, this new covenant was to bear the twin hallmarks of the old one. First, it would be *ratified in blood*. Not this time, however, the blood of some hapless animal but 'the precious blood of Christ, a lamb without blemish or defect' (1 Peter 1:18).

Second, the beneficiaries of the new covenant would be invited to a *meal* — the covenant meal, the Lord's Supper.

The stage set

To summarise, then: we have noted the importance of meals in Bible times among both Jews and pagans. We have observed how, far from just satisfying hunger, they were occasions for togetherness and mutual commitment. We have seen in particular how the partaking of a meal, along with the shedding of blood, used to set the seal on a covenant.

Hopefully, therefore, we can see how the scene was set, in both sacred and secular terms, for the institution by our Lord Jesus of that most significant religious meal of all, when he would announce, 'This cup is the new covenant in my blood.'

The Lord's Supper would arrive on the stage of history, not as some surprise 'special effect', but as the climax of a drama divinely scripted and produced so that the background, the scenery, the players and every previous act prepared the disciples, and after them the church in every age, for its momentous entry.

6

A prophetic drama

No one has ruined Shakespeare more than school-teachers.
I remember studying *King Lear*. By the time we had taken
it to bits, analysed the language, the characters and the plot,
the play was in pieces for me, a total ruin.

Things got put right when I went to a theatre and actually
saw the play. What a difference! I found myself drawn into
the unfolding plot, caught up with the powerful emotions
of the characters. I came away stirred; I had experienced *the
play as a whole*.

A play is something to be first and foremost experienced.
Study and analysis may help, but they are only means to an
end.

The same holds true for the Lord's Supper. We run the
danger of looking long and hard at every little detail of the
Bible accounts and, in so doing, missing its meaning as a
whole.

Two kinds of parable

The Lord's Supper, I suspect, is a simple parable rather than
an allegorical one. In an allegory every detail has some
meaning, like Jesus' story of the weeds where 'the one who
sowed the good seed is the Son of Man. The field is the world,
and the good seed stands for the sons of the kingdom. The
weeds are the sons of the evil one, and the enemy who sows

them is the devil. The harvest is the end of the age and the harvesters are angels' (Matthew 13:37-39).

A simple parable, on the other hand, has one main point only; the details are merely supportive and mustn't be pressed too far.

The story of the Good Samaritan has one simple message: be kind to all. We can do without the nonsensical interpretation of detail which assures us that the oil and wine are the Holy Spirit and joy, the donkey (with its four legs) is the four Gospels, the inn is the church and the two coins paid to the innkeeper are Bible-reading and prayer!

The Lord's Supper mustn't be pressed for too much detail either, or we shall end up reading things into it that aren't there. It stands in the biblical tradition of prophetic drama beloved of the Old Testament prophets. They didn't just say things, they *did* things! Jeremiah smashed clay pots (Jeremiah 19). Ezekiel shaved his head and burnt or scattered the hairs (Ezekiel 5). Isaiah walked around stripped and barefoot (Isaiah 20). Each had one straightforward message to convey in a dramatic way.

Jesus and prophetic drama

Towards the end of his ministry, Jesus employed prophetic drama, too. His triumphal entry into Jerusalem, his cleansing of the temple, his washing of the disciples' feet can all be seen in these terms.

It was never his intention, after the foot-washing, for the disciples to ask each other, 'Have we got a bowl and towel of the same colour and texture as the ones Jesus used? And let's see, now, did he wipe our feet in a clockwise or anticlockwise motion? We must get it right.'

He wasn't even saying that footwashing was obligatory; he said, 'I have set you an example that you should do as I have done for you' (John 13:15). *'As* I have done for you', not *'what* I have done for you'. The message of his prophetic action was simple: *serve* one another!

When we come to the Last Supper, therefore, we need to

stand back and look at it as a whole. What was uppermost in Jesus' mind as he instituted the feast? Clearly it was his imminent death, a death 'which is for you' (1 Corinthians 11:24).

His death was an *action,* and it was probably the whole *action* of giving them the bread and wine which we should see as symbolising that death, more than the details of the elements themselves. Nowhere, for example, does Scripture suggest that the act of breaking the bread represents the breaking of his body in crucifixion. 'To break bread' was the normal expression for 'to begin a meal'.

Jesus' emphasis, conveyed in the command *'Do* this', was on the whole action. 'I'm about to die,' he was saying. 'You can't grasp it yet, but there are ramifications to my death more than you could ever imagine. Later, you'll understand. When I'm gone, do this to bring it all to mind.'

And they did. Setting aside, then, our tendency to read into the details of the Last Supper what was probably never intended to be there, let's take the broader view appropriate to the simple parable. What *major* allusions would the act bring to the apostles' minds, in the light of their Jewish background, as they reclined with Jesus that night? They are two, and both would later be developed more fully in their writings under the illumination of the Holy Spirit.

The Passover connection

First, there was the obvious *Passover* connection, which we have examined already. A lamb was killed, God's wrath was averted, slavery was left behind and a new, free nation came into being.

Though that is quickly said, it makes the Christian's heart leap! He sees immediately that, in the same way, 'Christ, our Passover lamb, has been sacrificed' (1 Corinthians 5:7) and we are 'saved from God's wrath through him' (Romans 5:9). We have been bought out of slavery (redeemed) 'not with perishable things such as silver or gold . . . but with the precious blood of Christ, a lamb without blemish or defect' (1 Peter 1:18).

But what about a new, free nation coming into being? Is there a parallel there, too? Peter, James and John, at least, would have some light on this, because they would recall one incident which the other disciples hadn't been privileged to witness: the transfiguration.

On the mountain, you will recall, God had momentarily allowed them a glimpse behind the veil of Christ's humanity. They had seen Jesus shining with the divine glory that was properly his. And he had been joined there by Moses and Elijah, who also 'appeared in glorious splendour' (Luke 9:31).

So Moses, whom God had earlier forbidden from entering the promised land, had got in after all!

Moses had been the leader of the freed slaves in the great exodus from Egypt and now, on the Mount of Transfiguration, what was the subject of his conversation with Jesus and Elijah? They discussed another, greater exodus, one still to happen. They talked with Jesus 'about his departure (literally 'exodus') which he was about to bring to fulfilment at Jerusalem' (Luke 9:31).

So Jesus led an exodus, too? Yes indeed! After his crucifixion he marched out of the other side of death at the head of a mightier nation than ancient Israel. It was the new Israel, the church — a vast company of freed slaves, the redeemed community.

Dear old Peter had fumbled his conversation at the transfiguration (Luke 9:33), but he had obviously latched on to and understood the talk about Jesus' exodus. Later, he would take Old Testament scriptures originally spoken to Israel and apply them to the church, describing it as 'a chosen people, a royal priesthood, a *holy nation*, a people belonging to God' (1 Peter 2:9; Isaiah 43:20; Exodus 19:5-6).

Covenant associations

The Passover connection, then, was a major one. But there were also the great *covenant* associations of the Lord's Supper, which we considered earlier.

The old covenant had been ratified in blood, the blood of an animal, but the new covenant would require the blood of a victim more completely 'without defect' than any Passover lamb. Only the blood of the spotless Son of God could suffice to take away sin and write God's law on the hearts of men. That blood, the disciples began to realise as they listened to Jesus at the Last Supper, was about to be shed.

God had promised that, when the new covenant was ratified, he would 'forgive their wickedness and . . . remember their sins no more' (Jeremiah 31:34). Jeremiah had outlined the terms of the new covenant six centuries earlier but, like an unsigned document, it had stood without any binding power, awaiting the blood of ratification. With Jesus' own blood that covenant was about to be signed and brought into legal effect. Its sin-remitting power would soon be unleashed by that awsome signature.

Jesus said, 'This is my blood of the covenant, which is poured out for many for the forgiveness of sins' (Matthew 26:28). As the cup was passed round, did the disciples pick up the obvious reference to Isaiah's Suffering Servant of God who 'poured out his life unto death, and . . . bore the sins of many' (Isaiah 53:12)? Jesus himself was that Servant and his impending death would deal a fatal blow to the power of sin in human lives. In their lives. And in ours!

Keeping it simple

When I go away on a long overseas trip, my wife can finger her wedding ring and remember me. It reminds her of my vow to love her and be faithful to her, and my refusal even to think about divorce. It brings to mind the many happy times we have enjoyed together.

It is a token, too, of my assurance that I'll be on the plane home as soon as I can! To touch her ring, or even to look at it, conjures up a picture of love and togetherness.

Though the imagery is different, couched in terms of Passover and covenant, it is in this same simple, heartwarming way, I believe, that we should look upon the Lord's Supper.

7

The simple made complex

History has a way of complicating things. As the years of the Christian era rolled by, the simple act of sharing bread and wine, like any event repeated over a long period, took on board a number of complications.

Before looking at those complications, we must make the point that Jesus did intend the Lord's Supper to go on being observed. 'Do this', he commanded as he shared the bread and wine with his disciples (Luke 22:19). The use of the Greek present tense here implies 'Keep on doing this.'

Paul certainly saw it that way. And he took Christ's command to apply not just to the Twelve who had been present at the Last Supper but to all who honoured the name of Jesus. When he talks about 'the cup . . . for which we give thanks' and 'the bread that we break' (1 Corinthians 10:16), he implies that these were a regular feature of church life in Corinth, as they undoubtedly were elsewhere. The actual frequency of the meal is a matter we will return to later.

Like the Passover meal out of which it grew, the Lord's Supper began as a simple family meal or a meal shared by friends in a private house.

The believers in Jerusalem 'broke bread in their homes and ate together with glad and sincere hearts' (Acts 2:46). Where else could they do it? We mustn't forget that for at least the first hundred years of the church's existence there were no special church buildings. What's more, Christianity quickly became illegal, reinforcing the need to meet in the relative privacy of believers' houses.

The love-feast

The sharing of bread and wine took place, it would appear, *as part of a normal meal.* The expression 'break bread', as we have seen, commonly meant 'to begin a meal', but soon it attached itself to the sharing of bread and wine as distinct from the normal meal in the course of which it took place.

Meals have always been the best environment for the enjoyment of good fellowship — occasions for relaxation and conversation, where ideas and common interests are shared along with the food and drink. In the early church, the fellowship meal was called the *agapé* or love-feast (from the Greek *agapé,* meaning 'love'). We have a reference to such a meal in Jude 12, where certain troublemakers are called 'blemishes at your love-feasts'.

Similar meals took place in Corinth, and one of Paul's complaints is that the love-feasts there were badly named — they were lacking in love (see 1 Corinthians 11:17-22)! Some of the poorer believers were going without food altogether, while the wealthy ones were troughing away at the first century equivalent of smoked salmon and caviar, swilled down with *vin de table* till they were tipsy.

At some stage in the love-feast (probably at the beginning), there would be a conscious remembrance of Jesus with bread and wine, in obedience to his command. The whole affair, however, seems to have been marked at this early stage by easygoing spontaneity.

Gradually, changes came about. When church buildings began to figure in the picture, the Lord's Supper tended to be held there, rather than in the home. It is always more difficult to be relaxed in a public building, so a degree of formality inevitably crept in. The real meal — the *agapé* — faded out of the picture in the second century, leaving the symbolic meal only.

It was also inevitable, perhaps, that what went on inside the Christians' special buildings began to be influenced by the goings-on inside the pagan temples which were everywhere around (and possibly, in the case of converts from Judaism, by the temple ritual under the old covenant).

The standard elements of paganism were priests and sacrifices, splendour and ritual. In everyday thinking, no religion which lacked these elements stood much chance of popular acceptance. Sadly, they all left their mark on the Lord's Supper.

Emergence of the priesthood

With the passage of time, church elders came to be viewed as a priesthood, a privileged group serving as intermediaries between God and the people.

Now what use is a priest if he has no sacrifice to offer and no altar to offer it upon? Soon, therefore, altars began to appear in church buildings and the bread and wine came to be seen as a repetition of Christ's sacrifice, offered again to God. Candles appeared on the altar from around 1100 AD, with crucifixes following a hundred years later.

These developments ensured that, little by little, the role of the ordinary people underwent a change; instead of being participants, they became spectators, railed off from the altar where the priest performed his religious magic.

And magic it was, because the view gradually developed that by pronouncing the words 'This is my body . . . blood' the priest could effect a change of the bread and wine into the actual body and blood of Jesus (even though, mysteriously, their taste, smell and appearance remained unchanged). This change later came to be called *transubstantiation*.

It is interesting that the classical magician's words, 'Hocus pocus', come directly from *'Hoc est corpus meum'*, the Latin for 'This is my body' — Latin being until recently the worldwide language of the Roman Catholic Church.

If Jesus was indeed the King he claimed to be, then, it was argued, all the trappings of royalty needed bringing into the sacred building where, at the priest's word, he would regularly appear. Lavish and splendid decoration became the order of the day, a suitable setting for a formal ritual.

By this stage, even if some had *wanted* to celebrate the Lord's Supper informally, as at the beginning, the setting alone would have made it virtually impossible.

The pomp and ceremony, splendour and ritual, found their climax in the full-blown Roman Catholic mass, which remains to this day. In the East, a similar ritualism marked the Orthodox Church, where the change of the elements into the very body and blood of Christ were supposedly effected, not by the words of consecration, but by the *epiclesis* — the calling upon the Holy Spirit by the priest to bring it about.

Devotion diluted

Meanwhile, other changes were taking place in the background. Christianity became the official religion of the Roman Empire early in the fourth century. Soon, popularity blunted the sharp edge of living faith, hitherto kept finely honed by persecution. Many unregenerate people joined the church in order to further their career prospects or to keep up appearances.

When vital, living faith goes out of the window, formality and religious routine come in at the door. Church members who partook of the Lord's Supper out of genuine love for Jesus became a minority. Formal, liturgical procedures became the order of the day. ('Liturgy' means a set form of service.)

At the same time, what had started out as an act of pure devotion to Christ became bogged down in theological argument. Astute minds engaged in philosophical warfare over issues like the relationship between the bread/wine and the body/blood of the Lord.

As all these changes were taking place, the preaching and teaching of the Bible played a less and less important role in church life. Inevitably so. Why should people want to listen to preaching about Christ when Christ himself would show up in transubstantiated bread and wine whenever the priest pronounced the words of consecration?

It was a vicious circle, for the neglect of Scripture, in its turn, removed what little restraint remained on further ritualistic excesses.

The Reformation of the sixteenth century, with its return to the Bible, saw many of the mediaeval extremes corrected. But the ritualism of centuries had left its mark on the celebration of the Lord's Supper, and even many of the 'enlightened' groups settled for a form of celebration far removed from the warmth and spontaneity of the early church.

Terminology

Today's denominations represent different degrees of reform. That's why we find such widely varying practices as those I described in the opening chapter.

Even the terminology is varied. What I have called the *Lord's Supper* (on the strength of Paul's use of the term in 1 Corinthians 11:20) is alternatively called *communion* or, more commonly, holy communion. This term, traditionally favoured by Anglicans and some nonconformist denominations (that is, groups that are neither Roman Catholic nor Anglican), comes from the King James Version of 1 Corinthians 10:16: 'The cup of blessing which we bless, is it not the communion of the blood of Christ?'

Others prefer the *Lord's table* (1 Corinthians 10:21) or the *breaking of bread* (Acts 2:42), while Roman Catholics and 'high church' Anglicans prefer *mass*. This is not a biblical expression at all, coming from the Latin phrase, *'Ite, missa est'* ('Go, the congregation is dismissed'), spoken by the priest at the end of the service.

Another popular term among Anglicans, other than the 'high church' stream, is *eucharist,* a Greek-based term meaning 'thanksgiving' and used by Paul in the context of the Lord's Supper in 1 Corinthians 11:24: 'When (Jesus) had *given thanks,* he broke (the bread) . . . .'

Which term we use is of little importance, though, for myself, I prefer to avoid the ones with ritualistic overtones. In this book, therefore, I normally refer to the Lord's Supper.

To summarise, then: the Lord's Supper moved out of private houses into church buildings. Those buildings became ever more elaborate, and so did the ceremony which took place inside them, copying pagan practice. The real meal — the *agapé* — faded out in favour of the symbolic meal. Participation gave way to spectatorship.

Elders became priests, a body of 'clergy' set apart from the 'laity' and fitted by their 'ordination' to perform the miracle of transubstantiation. Living faith yielded to religious routine, and devotion to Christ was swept aside by theological argument. While much error has since been rectified, especially in the last four hundred years, the legacy of ritualism remains.

Speaking from a biblical standpoint, there is a strong case for arguing that the Lord's Supper is given too much importance in some quarters. The Roman Catholic and Eastern Orthodox churches, of course, see it as absolutely central. But even a Baptist order-book states that 'Christian worship is essentially eucharistic', while statements like 'The eucharist is the central act of Christian worship' go unchallenged.

Yes, whether we care to admit it or not, history has left its mark on our thinking. Letting go of our preconceived ideas is no easy business!

What do we eat and drink?

Our brief historical survey has highlighted the importance of the question: What exactly do we eat and drink at the Lord's Supper? Is it just bread and wine, or something more? The answer will expose our understanding of Jesus' words: 'This is my body . . . this is my blood' (Matthew 26:26, 28), and we must now examine this matter more closely.

In what sense are the elements his body and blood? Since, according to the Scripture record, it was ordinary Passover bread and a cup of everyday wine that Jesus handed to his disciples, it seems reasonable to see these as *tokens* or *symbols* of his body and blood. But literalists feel themselves to be on firm ground in insisting that that isn't what Jesus said. The words 'This *is* my body . . . blood,' they argue, mean exactly what they say.

'This *is* my body'

This literal view of things developed gradually over many centuries, as we have seen. Crude language quickly crept in, so that John Chrysostom (fourth century) could talk about eating the bread in terms of 'burying the teeth in his flesh'. The literalist approach, under the name of transubstantiation, received the final stamp of approval at a council of the church — the Fourth Lateran Council — in 1215 AD:

His body and blood are truly contained in the sacrament

of the altar under the appearance of bread and wine, the bread being transubstantiated into the body by the divine power and the wine into the blood.

Thomas Aquinas, a mediaeval theologian, explained transubstantiation in philosophical terms. These he borrowed from the pagan philosopher, Aristotle, who, as two modern writers explain, saw reality in terms of 'substance' and 'accidents':

A table is a table because it possesses the substance of 'tableness'. All tables possess this substance. That is why they are tables and are recognisable as such. But tables also possess accidents — size, shape, hardness, etc., and so many different kinds of tables exist. Their substance is the same, tableness, but their accidents are different. Similarly, bread is bread because it contains an invisible substance, 'breadness', and visible accidents — size, shape, taste, etc. Wine contains the substance of 'wineness' and accidents of colour and taste.[1]

When, according to Aquinas, the priest pronounced the words of consecration, a change came about in the bread and wine. But not a change in their accidents, only in their *substance*. Hence the term tran*substan*tiation.

Most ordinary people, of course, couldn't cope with this type of philosophical reasoning and took a more basic view of the change.

Some scholars who unquestionably did understand it doubted the doctrine just the same. John Wycliffe, who led a movement for reform within the Catholic Church in the fourteenth century, went to the heart of the issue. 'Mice,' he remarked (with a twinkle in his eye, I suspect), 'have an innate knowledge of the fact that the substance of bread is retained, as at first'!

Following hard on Wycliffe's heels came the sixteenth century Reformation, with its long-overdue return to biblical principles. When it questioned transubstantiation, the Roman Catholic Church replied with a Counter-Reformation, whose Council of Trent (1545-1563) reaffirmed the doctrine in stronger terms than ever. It still stands today.

Use of figurative language

The choice is plain: either there is a change in the bread and wine, or there isn't. If there isn't, no amount of church pronouncements can alter it. A plain look at Scripture points clearly in the direction of there being no change.

To begin with, Jesus was still in his body when he offered his disciples the bread and wine. His body and blood were one thing, the bread and wine another. What's more, the word 'is', upon which so much hangs in the statement 'This *is* my body . . . blood', doesn't appear in the Aramaic or Hebrew language which Jesus spoke. The nearest English equivalent would be, 'This my body . . . blood', or possibly, 'Behold, my body . . . blood'.

But even if we allow the word 'is' some value, its use (along with other forms of the verb 'to be') to link objects in a non-literal sense is commonplace. I show friends a photo of my wife and children with the words, 'This *is* my family.' Scripture, too, is full of examples: 'The field *is* the world' (Matthew 13:38); 'I *am* the gate' (John 10:7); 'the three baskets *are* three days' (Genesis 40:18); 'this *is* Jerusalem' (Ezekiel 5:5).

Essentially, the Passover wasn't a meal but an act of divine judgment, yet God himself said of the meal which signified it, 'It *is* the Lord's Passover' (Exodus 12:11). To this day, whenever Jews celebrate that feast, the head of the family breaks bread with the words, 'This is the bread of affliction which our fathers ate when they left Egypt.' No-one is foolish enough to say, 'How come it's not mouldy by now if it's so old?'

At his celebration of the Passover at the Last Supper, Jesus used a similar figure of speech: 'This cup is the new covenant in my blood' (Luke 22:20). Everybody agrees that the word 'is' here can only mean 'represents'. Why, then, should he not have been using the same figure when he said, 'This is my body . . . blood'?

God frequently uses signs. Even back in Egypt, the Hebrew slaves preparing for the exodus were told, 'The blood will be a *sign* for you' (Exodus 12:13). The normal use of language, the standard principles of biblical interpretation and sanctified common sense all indicate, then, that the bread and wine are exactly that — signs, and no more.

Consubstantiation

At the Reformation, Martin Luther and his followers came up with a modified view of transubstantiation know as consubstantiation. After consecration by the priest the bread and wine remain, they taught, but the flesh and blood of Christ co-exist in them and with them. Just as an iron bar, when heated in a flame, remains an iron bar, but with the new element of heat in it, so the flesh and blood of Christ co-exist with the bread and wine.

It's a clever idea, but in some ways even harder for the ordinary mind to grasp than transubstantiation. In any case, the argument for both doctrines depends on two non-biblical assumptions: first, that there are certain 'words of consecration' which can bring about a change in the elements, and, second, that there is a priesthood qualified by ordination to speak those words.

Both doctrines, as we have seen, lack biblical support. As they collapse, therefore, the doctrines of both transubstantiation and consubstantiation, which ride on their shoulders, collapse with them.

The idea of sacrifice

Priests and altars, of course, go hand-in-hand with sacrifices. Is the Lord's Supper in any sense a sacrifice?

In the second century, Athenagoras replied to the charges of atheism being levelled by pagans against Christians on the grounds that they had neither priests nor altars. He pointed out that you need neither of these items to know God. It wasn't long, however, before both appeared as a rub-off from paganism, and with them came the notion of sacrifice.

The sacrificial idea attached itself specifically to the Lord's Supper, which was renamed the mass and seen as 'an unbloody sacrifice for the sins of the living and the dead'.

The whole concept runs counter to the plain teaching of the Bible. What value can there be in an 'unbloody sacrifice' when Scripture declares that 'without the shedding of blood there is no forgiveness' (Hebrews 9:22)? In any case, there is no further need for sacrifices, bloody or otherwise, since Jesus has 'offered for all time *one* sacrifice for sins' (Hebrews 10:12). Scripture hammers home the 'once for all' nature of Christ's sacrifice again and again (Hebrews 7:27; 9:12, 26; 10:12, 17-18; John 19:30; 1 Peter 3:18).

We do well to note, however, that Scripture speaks of two kinds of sacrifice. There is the *propitiatory* kind, which appeases God's wrath and secures mercy and forgiveness for sin. Such was Christ's unique self-sacrifice. Because of its complete and final nature, there can be no further sacrifices of this kind.

There is also the *non-propitiatory* kind. This is the sacrifice of praise, the offering by the redeemed of all that they are and have in gratitude and worship to the Lord who saved them. Sacrifices of this kind go on daily.

As 'a holy priesthood, offering spiritual sacrifices acceptable to God through Jesus Christ' (1 Peter 2:5), we Christians offer our *bodies* as living sacrifices (Romans 12:1), especially our *voices* as instruments of praise (Hebrews 13:15). We offer *ourselves as agents of the gospel* (see Romans 15:15; 2 Timothy 4:5-6). Our time and effort put into *mutual caring,* as well as our gifts of *money* for the Lord's work, are sacrifices with which God is pleased (Hebrews 13:16; Philippians 4:18).

Roman Catholicism, however, insists on putting the Lord's Supper firmly in the first category, declaring, in the words of the Council of Trent, 'This sacrifice is truly propitiatory.' Such a view Scripture plainly forbids.

If the Lord's Supper has sacrificial connections at all, it is to be compared not to a sacrifice at an altar but to the meal which customarily followed a sacrifice and was celebrated at a table with food and drink — in this case a sequel to, not a repeat of, the 'once for all' sacrifice of Jesus.

In that sense the Lord's Supper can legitimately be viewed as part of the sacrifice of praise. Our celebration of it is an act of obedience by which we joyfully worship the one who left the command, 'Do this'.

Chapter 8 NOTES
1. D. Bridge & D. Phypers, *The Meal that Unites?* Hodder & Stoughton, 1981, p76

9

Eating his flesh, drinking his blood

If the Lord's Supper is, as we suggested earlier, a prophetic drama with a simple message of covenant faithfulness and freedom from slavery, is there any more particular sense in which we can talk of eating Christ's flesh and drinking his blood?

The answer must be yes, if only because Jesus himself said, 'Unless you can eat the flesh of the Son of Man and drink his blood, you have no life in you' (John 6:53).

A large part of this sixth chapter of John's Gospel is given over to the flesh-eating and blood-drinking theme, and it is inconceivable that the apostles would have failed to connect it with the Lord's Supper. Certainly the connection has been made by Christians in every generation since. So what are we to make of it?

If you aren't familiar with John 6, it would be helpful to pause right now and read it through. The chapter's outline is simple enough: Everything began when Jesus provided bread and fish for the five thousand. Soon, a debate was in progress about his claim to be manna personified, 'the living bread that came down from heaven' (v51). The debate moved into the synagogue at Capernaum, and further explanation was later given privately to the disciples.

We can hardly blame the Jews, or the disciples, for their puzzlement and shock at the idea of eating flesh and drinking blood. It is an appalling enough concept to us — a generation whose horror films make *Frankenstein* look tame. But for Jews, the consumption of blood was doubly appalling. Not only was it a natural turn-off; it was also an abomination from the religious standpoint, expressly forbidden by Leviticus 17:10-12. And to their literalist minds, statements like, 'If anyone eats of this bread, he will live for ever. This bread is my flesh, which I will give for the life of the world' (v51) must have smacked of cannibalism!

Jesus' statements at the Last Supper are no less shocking if we view them in this same literal way: 'Take and eat; this is my body' and 'Drink from it, all of you. This is my blood of the covenant' (Matthew 26:26-28).

We can hardly blame the Jews for asking each other, *'How can this man give us his flesh to eat?'* (John 6:52). Happily, Jesus gave some conclusive answers to that question.

Eating is believing

To begin with, Jesus knocks crude literalism on the head. The feasting in question, he says, is a *spiritual* feasting, not a fleshly one: 'The Spirit gives life; the flesh counts for nothing. The words I have spoken to you' — all this talk about flesh-eating and blood-drinking — 'are spirit and they are life' (v63).

Physical bread, he says, is 'food that spoils' (v27). If left, it will soon go mouldy and rot. We are to work not primarily for that kind of food, Jesus goes on, 'but for *food that endures to eternal life,* which the Son of Man will give you' (v27). So this must be non-physical food, the kind that doesn't go rotten in a few days. It is spiritual food, something eaten not with the mouth but with the heart.

This is exactly what Jesus confirms: 'He who *comes* to me will never go hungry, and he who *believes* in me will never be thirsty' (v35). *To eat his flesh and drink his blood, then, is to come to him and believe in him* — nothing more and nothing less.

There are more vital appetites, he is saying, than those

marked by a shrunken stomach and a parched throat. In the final analysis, it is the hunger and thirst of the spirit that will prove to be of more lasting importance. And while he is concerned that we have food and drink of the everyday kind — isn't that why he fed the five thousand? — he longs to meet our spiritual needs, too.

Physical needs are met by physical eating and drinking; spiritual needs are met by spiritual eating and drinking — that is, by our coming to him and putting our trust in him.

The correctness of this view is confirmed when we look at the *benefits* of eating and drinking. Jesus promises, 'Whoever eats my flesh and drinks my blood *has eternal life, and I will raise him up at the last day*' (v54).

These twin blessings — eternal life now and a physical resurrection at the day of judgment — are familiar New Testament promises.

When we look outside of John 6 to see what other terms Scripture uses to describe how we receive them, we discover that, in line with John 6, it is by coming to Jesus and believing in him: 'The Son of Man must be lifted up, that everyone who *believes in him* may have eternal life' (John 3:15). 'I am the resurrection and the life. He who *believes in me* will live, even though he dies' (John 11:25).

Let's settle this in our minds, then. To eat Christ's flesh and drink his blood is picture language for coming to him in living faith.

Yet we dare not say that his flesh and blood are not *real* food and drink, because, in the strict sense, eternal, spiritual, unseen things are more 'real' than things visible and physical (2 Corinthians 4:18). 'Real' and 'literal' are not the same thing. When Jesus says, 'My flesh is *real* food and my blood is *real* drink' (v55) he means that, unlike wholemeal bread and French wine, they last for ever; believing in him has eternal consequences.

Believing is seeing

Feeding on Christ, then, means believing in him. But what

does it mean to believe? This is not the silly question it may seem, for the word 'believe' is used in a variety of ways.

For Jesus' immediate audience in John 6, believing meant their seeing beyond the ordinary-looking man who sat under a tree talking to them, and recognising the incarnate Son of God whose mission was to give himself for the sins of the world. But their short-sighted vision didn't stretch that far. 'Is this not Jesus, the son of Joseph,' they muttered, 'whose father and mother we know?' (v42).

For us, living later in history, believing means the same as for them: seeing Jesus for who he truly is — not just a great teacher but God manifest in the flesh — and being quick to draw close to put our faith in him, and so to satisfy the inner hunger of our souls.

That hunger will never be satisfied, however, by mere admiration of his great and noble example. It can find satisfaction only in his death on the cross. His wonderful sinless life was only a preliminary to his atoning death, without which there could be no resurrection or ascension, no poured-out Spirit, no new covenant, no personal salvation and no New Testament church. 'This bread,' he explained, hinting at his forthcoming sacrifice, 'is my flesh, *which I will give for the life of the world*' (v51).

Our believing — our spiritual eating and drinking — must embrace Calvary, where his blood was shed and his flesh mutilated, yet seeing beyond his physical wounds to the spiritual miracle: the bearing away of our sins.

Eating that continues

Our believing, too, must be more than a one-off act of personal commitment to him.

Though it begins that way, the spiritual life is 'from faith to faith' (Romans 1:17 NASB). We *keep on* feeding upon him. Our hearts, which reached out to him in faith at the beginning, hold on to him in a faith that continues. Like Simon Peter, we tell Jesus we can't leave him because we have no-one else to go to: 'You have the words of eternal

life. We believe and know that you are the Holy One of God'
(v68-69).

To continue trusting him this way is what it means to go
on feeding upon him, to continue eating his flesh, so to speak,
and drinking his blood: 'Whoever eats (literally: goes on
eating) my flesh and drinks (literally: goes on drinking) my
blood remains in me, and I in him' (v56).

In taking the bread and wine of the Lord's Supper, then,
we make a pledge of continuing trust in Jesus and his death
for us. The bread is just bread, the wine just wine, but the
eye of faith sees them in spiritual terms. As we eat and drink,
chew and swallow, we say to Jesus, 'Lord, I'm continuing
to trust you for everything.'

God's own provision

It was mention of the manna in the wilderness, you will
remember, that first prompted the teaching of John 6. The
manna eaten by the Israelites was physical food, with
nutritional value. Likewise, the water from the rock was
genuine, with thirst-quenching properties. Why, then, does
Paul call them 'spiritual food' and 'spiritual drink' (1
Corinthians 10:3-4)?

He calls them 'spiritual' because they were the provision
of God, a daily token of his covenant love towards his people.

In a similar sense we can say that the bread and wine of
communion are also spiritual food and drink. Physically they
may be Allinson's Stoneground and Hirondelle Medium Red,
but to us they are tokens of God's provision for our spiritual
needs in the person of Christ. As we feed upon them with
our mouths and stomachs, we feed upon Christ in our hearts
by faith, and we are thankful.

Sinless life, atoning death

Food is what sustains life. Stop eating, and we die. 'I have
food to eat that you know nothing about,' said Jesus to his
disciples on one occasion. They imagined (of course!) that
he had a private pantry somewhere. But he explained: 'My

food is to do the will of him who sent me' (John 4:32-34). The thing that kept Jesus going, at a deeper level than filling his stomach, was *doing God's will*. His life of sinless obedience was a testimony to his regular 'eating' of his Father's commands (see Jeremiah 15:16).

And what of his drinking? The cup in Scripture often symbolises the wrath of God. 'Rise up, O Jerusalem,' says Isaiah, 'you who have drunk from the hand of the Lord *the cup of his wrath*, you who have drained to its dregs the goblet that makes men stagger' (Isaiah 51:17).

'Can you drink the cup I drink?' Jesus once asked the disciples (Mark 10.38). Though they would have their share of sufferings for his sake, they could never drink the cup of God's wrath in quite the way he did. This was the cup of death, of hell and of divine judgment upon sin which horrified him in Gethsemane. 'Take this cup from me,' he begged his Father, adding, in line with his pattern of determined submission, 'Yet not what I will, but what you will' (Mark 14:36).

In life Jesus fed on obedience to God's will. In death he drained the cup of God's wrath. Whenever *we* eat and drink at the Lord's Supper we enter into a new appreciation of those two things: his spotless life, and his atoning death on our behalf.

Grace before eating

We remember with gratitude, too, that we stand as beneficiaries of Christ's death purely by God's grace. Attendance at the Lord's Supper is not, as some teach, a 'work', a means of stacking up spiritual credit.

We return to John 6 to notice that, in the context of eating and drinking, of coming to him and believing, Jesus states, 'No-one can come to me unless the Father has enabled him' (v65). Pride and self-righteousness wilt before that statement. 'From this time,' John records, 'many of his disciples turned back and no longer followed him' (v66).

We who have come and believed, however, rejoice that

grace alone made it possible. Every time we take bread and wine, the physical tokens of our trust in him, we celebrate God's grace. 'Father,' we cry, 'we're here as your children, your very own. What love you have lavished on us, that we should be called children of God. And that is what we are! *You* did it, Father. Your grace is wonderful!

'Jesus, you loved us and gave yourself for us. We celebrate your grace — that though you were rich, yet for our sakes you became poor, so that we through your poverty might become rich. And here we are, rich beyond compare.

'*You* did it, Jesus. We love you. We worship you. Your grace is amazing!'

10

Who's
for supper?

The cross has a horizontal bar as well as an upright. And the covenant sealed at the cross of Christ has horizontal as well as vertical implications.

'God . . . loved us,' says John, 'and sent his Son as an atoning sacrifice for our sins' (1 John 4:10). That's the vertical aspect of the covenant — our corporate relationship with God. The horizontal aspect follows on from it and appears in the very next verse: 'Dear friends, since God so loved us, we also ought to love one another.'

The argument is devastatingly simple: if you belong to God, and I belong to God, then you and I belong to each other. We don't choose our brothers; God chooses them for us. We are joined under the covenant.

The Lord's Supper, being the covenant meal, is intended *for members of the covenant community*. Only those who have eaten Christ's flesh and drunk his blood in the John 6 sense of coming to him and putting their trust in him are qualified to eat the Lord's Supper.

In Old Testament days, of course, the people of Israel were the covenant community, but since the ratification of the new covenant by Christ's death and resurrection, that has changed. God's new 'holy nation' is the church, and the promises made to Israel have become the church's property. That much Paul makes clear when, quoting a string of such promises, he says to the ex-pagans of Corinth, 'Since *we* have these promises, dear friends . . .' (2 Corinthians 7:1).

The covenant meal, then, is for covenant people, members of the church. But I must make it clear what I mean by 'church'. I don't mean the lumbering denominational institutions which are the residue of history. The church is the sum total of the elect, the redeemed community, the body of beneficiaries of the new covenant, those whose names are written in heaven.

Celebrating the meal in terms of the church universal — the world-wide company of believers — can pose problems. While there are undoubted blessings in sharing bread and wine with a fellow-Christian you have never met before and may never meet again, there are also limitations. You can rejoice in being brothers or sisters in the Lord, but circumstances don't allow you any regular, practical opportunity to demonstrate your brotherhood.

The traditional barriers raised by history between genuine Christians of different persuasions can also make communion difficult.

The charismatic renewal began to break down some of those barriers, though there has been some recent rehardening of denominational attitudes. At the united praise meetings and conferences which were once commonplace, whenever the Lord's Supper came up for united celebration, some of the old barriers proved insurmountable, even if only between the charismatic Catholics and the rest. Either the Supper was tactfully omitted or groups of believers, 'all one in Christ Jesus', made their way from united sessions into separate rooms to 'take holy communion', 'remember the Lord', 'attend mass', 'celebrate the eucharist' or 'break bread' according to their various traditions.

Covenant in the local church

The *local* church is a far better context for working out the covenant horizontally. The members live in the same geographical area; they see each other regularly; they recognise the same church leadership; they have a working relationship. 'We belong to each other' makes practical sense and the sharing of the Lord's Supper is therefore warm and meaningful.

Within the local church, or even across local church boundaries, smaller groups (like the Twelve at the Last Supper) will also eat the covenant meal. Housegroups and common-interest groups such as children's workers, musicians or street-evangelism units may see it as a way of strengthening their relationship.

And as part of a local church, Christian families, too, will eat it. When a family all love the Lord, there is something peculiarly precious in husband, wife and children firming up their family bonds in Christ by the sharing of bread and wine.

Now we must return to the question of definitions. If the universal church is *the* community of the redeemed, the sum total of the elect in every place, then the local church is *a* community of the redeemed. This is certainly the biblical picture. The merely religious and other hangers-on may well attend some meetings, but by scriptural definition they aren't part of the church.

The local church is a mini-society within society, living under a different King and by higher standards. And who is responsible to see that it lives up to its definition? While that responsibility falls to a degree upon every member, it falls primarily upon the leaders.

The Eastern shepherd in Bible times, having gathered his flock into the sheepfold for the night, would lie down across the narrow entrance. He himself was the gate, protecting the sheep inside and barring the way to predators. Jesus, the great Shepherd, described himself in these very terms when he said, 'I am the gate for the sheep' (John 10:7).

Local church leaders are under-shepherds patterned on the pastoral leadership of Jesus himself (Acts 20:28-31) and, like him, they are the gate to the local church, responsible for ensuring the integrity of the flock.

Local church purity

Maintaining that purity means, first of all, *refusing to recognise obvious non-believers as part of the committed body,* and admitting only born-again believers to the covenant meal. But shouldn't the wheat and tares be left to grow together? No; the field is the world, not the church (Matthew 13:38).

The Passover regulation was clear: 'No foreigner is to eat of it' (Exodus 12:43). The meal was only for the covenant people, those sheltering behind the blood of the Passover lamb. It drew a bold line between insiders and outsiders as a meal at which 'the Lord makes a distinction between Egypt and Israel' (Exodus 11:7). That distinction was in line with the covenant sign of circumcision. 'No uncircumcised male may eat of it' (Exodus 12:48).

The parallels in the nation of the new covenant are obvious. Only those who have a personal stake in the shed blood of God's Lamb, Jesus, are part of the covenant people and qualified thereby to partake of the Lord's Supper.

That Supper is not something we just talk about, a mere doctrine or something of academic interest only; it is an *experience.* We actually put bread and wine in our mouths and swallow them. In doing so we demonstrate that Jesus is more to us than a figure of history or theology; we have personally met him, we have a living *experience* of him. Only those with the experience of Christ qualify for the experience of the Supper.

Old covenant circumcision of the flesh is replaced in the new by circumcision of the heart (Romans 2:28-29), and this is expressed by the new covenant sign of baptism (Colossians 2:11-12). The Lord's Supper is for the baptised.

Since the New Testament doesn't conceive of such a thing as an unbaptised believer, neither should we. Believers' baptism by immersion is not an option but part of the gospel (Acts 2:38). In fulfilling their evangelistic and pastoral responsibilities, local church leaders could do far worse than follow the example of Peter, who took an uncompromising line with those who had put their faith in Jesus: he *'ordered* that they be baptised' (Acts 10:48).

No, I'm not advocating the church equivalent of a military dictatorship! But much traditional church life, especially in Britain, has become so bland, so namby-pamby and indecisive, that there is a major need to return to the more gutsy approach of the church leaders in the New Testament, men like Paul and Peter, Timothy and James.

Though they had been broken by the cross of their Lord, they had also been touched by his Spirit. They were men of steel and velvet, men of conviction and of sympathy, men of decision and of understanding, men of firmness and of love. Where are such leaders today?

It must be stressed, in the light of the common (and harmful) practice of infant baptism, that whereas old covenant circumcision was for babies in the natural sense, new covenant baptism is for babies in the spiritual sense — those just born *again,* regardless of their natural years.

So the local church is *by definition* a blood-bought community, a people individually born again and baptised in water and the Spirit. The unregenerate are simply not part of it. While they may, and often will, attend some of the church's gatherings (1 Corinthians 14:23), they remain unqualified to take the Lord's Supper, and this should be explained to them in a warm and gracious manner. What an opportunity to urge them to come to Christ!

The dropping-off of unbelievers will often take place spontaneously. A healthy body has its own way of expelling foreign matter; a splinter embedded in the flesh is eventually pushed to the surface and out. So it is with a healthy spiritual body. The gifts of discernment, prophecy and the word of knowledge, as well as the experience of maturer Christians, will quickly expose professing members who are merely going through the motions.

Indeed, the very presence and power of God, living among his people by his Spirit, will deter unregenerate hangers-on. While we yearn for the freshness and vitality of the early church, we do well to remember that it comes as part of a package with the searching and burning aspects of God's presence. A 'mixed' church cannot remain mixed for long when God moves upon it in power.

The paradox of the early church was that because of the evident power of the Holy Spirit among them, 'no-one else dared join them'. And yet, 'more and more men and women believed in the Lord and were added to their number' (Acts 5:13-14).

Today, in countries with a long Christian history, such as Britain and the USA, a high proportion of local churches are of the 'mixed' variety. That must surely change.

Let us pray for such a powerful visitation of God that a radical polarisation will take place, enabling us to say of some, 'They went out from us, but they did not really belong to us. For if they had belonged to us, they would have remained with us; but their going showed that none of them belonged to us' (1 John 2:19). At the same time, let us open our arms wide to receive those whom the Lord himself will save and add to our numbers!

Judgment within the church

The maintenance of the local church's purity also requires that we *deal with sin in its members*. What is the point of calling ourselves a 'holy nation' if we aren't holy in practice?

After Israel's idolatrous worship of the golden calf, Moses issued his rallying call: 'Whoever is for the Lord, come to me' (Exodus 32:26). The repentant Levites rallied to him and were despatched throughout the camp to strike down their unrepentant fellow-Israelites.

A similar, though less drastic, event marked the restoration under Ezra, when Israelite men who had married foreign women were called to put them away (Ezra 9-10).

The reason for this kind of self-judgment is obvious: if we ourselves don't judge sin within the covenant community, God will do it for us — and those with a proper fear of the Lord will know which is the safer option! Ezra's officials dealt with the marriage issue promptly, determined to stay with it 'until the fierce anger of our God in this matter is turned away from us' (Ezra 10:14).

The same holds good in the church. 'If we judged ourselves,' explains Paul in the context of the Lord's Supper, 'we would not come under (God's) judgment' (1 Corinthians 11:31). On that basis, he urges: *'Keep away from* every brother who is idle and does not live according to the teaching you received from us' (2 Thessalonians 3:6).

When Paul discovered that the Corinthians were putting up with gross immorality in the church, the treatment he prescribed was drastic: *'Expel* the wicked man from among you' (1 Corinthians 5:13). They were to drive him out from under the umbrella of covenant fellowship into the cold and wet of Satan's territory, in the hope that he would soon feel lonely and chilly enough to repent of his sin and so qualify for readmission — which he apparently did (2 Corinthians 2:5-11).

Obviously, such drastic treatment is the last resort, not the first! More often than not, a situation will never reach this stage. Personal, private confrontation by another individual is the first step, followed by further confrontation in the presence of one or two witnesses. Only if, after all this, the sinful member still refuses to admit his fault and repent should the issue be brought before the church as a whole and, as a final step, the person be expelled (Matthew 18:15-17).

For all who seek to order their lives by the Word of God, such judgment by the local church of its own members is not optional; it is mandatory. By purifying itself, the local church is constantly striving to live up to God's ideal for it as a blood-bought, holy community. There is no room for easygoing complacency, let alone for Corinthian-style boasting.

'Your boasting is not good,' Paul chides them. 'Don't you know that a little yeast (sin) works through the whole batch of dough (the whole church)? Get rid of the old yeast that

you may be a new batch without yeast — *as you really are.*
For Christ, our Passover lamb, has been sacrificed. Therefore
let us keep the Festival, not with the old yeast, the yeast of
malice and wickedness, but with bread without yeast, the
bread of sincerity and truth' (1 Corinthians 5:6-8).

Here Paul is making a clear connection between the
Passover-Lord's Supper and the local church's judgment of
the incestuous man. Notice the words I have highlighted with
italics. 'Be what you are,' Paul is saying to the Corinthian
believers. 'Live up to the ideal of a pure and holy church,
which is what Christ died for. The responsibility is yours.'

Let him have the final word on the subject: 'I have written
to you in my letter *not to associate* with sexually immoral
people — not at all meaning the people of this world who
are immoral, or the greedy and swindlers, or idolaters. In
that case you would have to leave this world.

'But now I am writing to you that you must *not associate*
with anyone who calls himself a brother but is sexually
immoral or greedy, an idolater or a slanderer, a drunkard
or a swindler. *With such a man do not even eat.* What business
is it of mine to judge those outside? *Are you not to judge those
inside?* God will judge those outside' (1 Corinthians 5:9-13).

The public expulsion of an unrepentant member of the
church is a sobering business. Though the number of cases
I have been involved with over many years of pastoral
ministry could be counted on one hand, each one has caused
me pain, tears and loss of sleep. It has also brought a godly
sobriety upon the church (1 Timothy 5:20). We have realised
again that there is a world of difference between belonging
to the church of God and being a member of the Labour
Party, the Rotarians or the local Rugby club.

This is no 'easy come, easy go' situation. To be part of
the covenant community is a high and holy calling, with
immense privileges — and responsibilities to match.

No room for penance

Lest traditional values weigh upon our thinking, it needs to be said that the judging of unrepentant church members will mean more than banning them from taking the bread and wine.

In my Brethren days it was common for a form of penance to be exacted of wayward members; they would be asked to 'sit behind' and not partake of the elements when they came round. Apart from that, everything continued as usual. They attended all the meetings; they enjoyed the same hospitality, meal-sharing and fellowship; they were as much 'in' as before. Only the bread and wine were withheld for a specified number of weeks, in line with the gravity of the sin.

We must understand, though, that the Lord's Supper is only one visible expression — albeit an important one — of the covenant fellowship which has a thousand and one other expressions. The member who, when confronted with his sin, refuses to repent, must be put out of fellowship *altogether.* He will be unwelcome at any meetings or at the homes of members. All meals, outings and general hobnobbing will be closed to him.

Since the church is not where we go but what we are, there is far more to fellowship than the Lord's Supper — or church meetings in general, for that matter.

If, on the other hand, he is genuinely repentant, the church must receive him into their hearts and lives as before. The New Testament has no room for penances. Requiring him to sit at the back when the Lord's Supper is celebrated, morosely passing on the bread and wine without partaking, is a religious farce. Token judgment is a mockery; judgment must be real.

What a joy it is to receive a repentant member back into the bosom of the local church after expulsion! Since the expulsion was done publicly, the welcoming back must be public, too. There won't be a single dry eye in the place. Weeping for joy will be the order of the day!

This, then, is the background of church life and practice against which we must view the Lord's Supper. We are to ensure that the local church — the covenant community —

is a community of the redeemed. And we are to be lovingly firm in judging sin among its members. By these means we shall ensure that the Lord's Supper truly is the covenant meal.

11

Frequency
and conduct

Having settled the question of who is qualified to eat the covenant meal, we shall look in this chapter at some other questions commonly asked in connection with its celebration, beginning with the matter of frequency.

How often should we take the bread and wine?

The Passover feast out of which the Lord's Supper grew was an annual celebration, specifically designated as such by the Lord himself. But he has given no such ruling on the new covenant ordinance. Indeed, the pages of the New Testament are non-committal on the matter.

Jesus' words, 'Do this, whenever you drink it . . .' (1 Corinthians 11:25), and Paul's 'The cup of thanksgiving for which we give thanks . . . the bread that we break . . .' (1 Corinthians 10:16), both hint strongly at regular observance. In Jerusalem they broke bread 'every day' (Acts 2:46). (Though it isn't clear in the NIV translation, in the Greek the phrase 'every day' governs *all* the activities listed in that verse.)

Traditionally, it has become a weekly celebration, on a Sunday. Interestingly enough, recent research has shown that the Jewish 'cup of thanksgiving' wasn't confined to the annual Passover feast; it was drunk at a communal meal every sabbath.[1] This fact may partly account for the traditional pattern of weekly celebration of the Lord's Supper.

A weekly feast?

Our interest, though, is not in tradition, however ancient, but in the New Testament's guidelines. There are hints there that the first day of the week held special significance for the early church (Acts 20:7; 1 Corinthians 16:2). This is possibly because it was the day on which Jesus rose from the dead (Matthew 28:1-2), though Scripture nowhere specifically connects the two.

In all likelihood it was the first day of the week that John referred to in the phrase 'the Lord's day' in Revelation 1:10 — the only occurrence of this expression in Scripture. Barclay explains: 'In each Roman week there was a day called the Emperor's Day, and it was very natural for the Christians to have their Lord's Day. And what most likely happened was that the Lord's Day, so to speak, took the Lord's Supper with it, and the two became weekly together.'[2]

We must remember that, for over three centuries of the Christian era, Sunday was as much a normal working day for believers as it was for everyone else. It was the sun-worshipping Emperor Constantine who decreed in 321 AD that everyone 'should rest on the most honourable day of the sun'.

Idleness was thus legally enforced on the whole population, providing an ideal opportunity for the Christians to meet for worship. Such is the origin of our modern Sunday.

But worship isn't a one-day-in-seven affair, and every Christian worth the name identifies with the words of George Herbert's hymn:

> *Seven whole days, not one in seven,*
> *I will praise thee.*

If we are more holy on Sundays than on the other six days, we are only one seventh as holy as we ought to be. And if every day is appropriate for praising God, it is also appropriate for celebrating the Lord's Supper. The Christians in Jerusalem celebrated daily and so, if we wish, may we.

Beyond this, Scripture has little light to shed on the frequency question. Clearly we are left a great deal of flexibility, though as Howard Marshall points out, 'The fact that the Supper is a repeated occurrence indicates the continual dependence of the believer on Jesus'[3] — a good enough reason, surely, for frequent participation!

Time of day seems unimportant. Certainly there is no particular virtue in rising at some unearthly hour for the purpose, as if attendance at 'early communion' scored more credits that attendance mid-morning. As we have seen, the idea of credit doesn't come into it at all.

The expression 'the Lord's *Supper*' probably comes from its institution by Jesus at an evening meal, though there seems no reason why this should be seen as a better time than any other for celebrating it today.

The bread

What kind of bread and wine should we use?

The arguments for the use of unleavened bread will not stand scrutiny. It was certainly unleavened bread that Jesus broke at the Last Supper, because that was specified for the Passover (Exodus 12:8). But Christians aren't bound by Passover restrictions. If we keep that feast at all, it is in a spiritual sense, and the Festival of Unleavened Bread has a *moral* application: 'Christ, our Passover lamb, has been sacrificed. Therefore let us keep the Festival, not with the old yeast, the yeast of malice and wickedness, but with bread without yeast, *the bread of sincerity and truth*' (1 Corinthians 5:7-8).

What matters, in other words, is how we live. Whether our bread is leavened or unleavened is irrelevant. Normal bread in Western countries is leavened, and that is what we will customarily use.

I say 'normal bread'. The preparation of special bread or wafers for exclusive use at the Lord's Supper is neither necessary nor desirable. Such a practice only heightens the mystique of celebration in a way which runs counter to the spiritual informality which God intended for the meal.

Should the bread be broken at the time of participating or cubed beforehand?

Again, it doesn't matter. A point against the practice of pre-cubing or using individual wafers, however, is Paul's lesson on Christian unity in the local church, drawn from the analogy of 'the one loaf' (1 Corinthians 10:17). More on this later.

As befits normal bread, it ought not to be treated with any more respect than the bread in the pantry. The placing of it on a special table carved with Bible texts, the use of a silver plate, the covering of it with a fancy cloth — all these are unnecessary complications, though a cloth could be useful if there are flies about.

Nor is there any reason why any bread remaining after the meal shouldn't be spread with butter and jam and eaten later, or dropped in the waste-bin, or scattered on the local duck-pond. It isn't holy bread. It's just bread.

The wine

And the wine — should it be alcoholic or not?

Red wine (symbolic of blood) was traditionally specified for the Passover and, being normal wine, it was of the fermented kind. Again, the principle of normality would suggest ordinary red wine for the Lord's Supper. Some may prefer unfermented grape juice or some other substitute, especially if there are converted alcoholics in the church. It makes little difference what we choose.

Should we have one shared cup or individual mini-cups?

Paranoia over hygiene (heightened by the AIDS scare) has put many off the use of a common cup. This has to be weighed against the powerful symbolism of sharing the same cup — an expression of our common dependence on the blood of Christ and our resultant unity — though it has to be said that this isn't stressed by Paul in the same way as he stresses the symbolic meaning of the one loaf.

In his recent book on AIDS, Dr Patrick Dixon looks carefully at the supposed risks with the communion cup and concludes: 'The communion cup is safe and I will continue to drink from it. We are not going to see a great epidemic of AIDS through church congregations because of the communion cup! It just will not and cannot happen.'[4]

Some churches pass round a cloth with the cup so that each drinker can wipe the rim before passing it on.

If we go for a single cup, what sort should it be?

The obvious answer is a normal wineglass. But since that would in many cases be too small, something larger may be called for. Special chalices, made of silver or some other expensive material and inscribed with religious symbols such as a cross or the chi-rho monogram, are not intrinsically wrong. But in the constant struggle against ritual and formality they are probably unhelpful.

Who takes charge?

Who should preside over the dispensing of the bread and wine?

Tradition is quick to rear its ugly head here. Those whose immediate response is 'A priest' or 'An ordained minister' should remember our determination to lean only on Scripture, where neither of these categories figures at all.

Whatever their function in the church, Christians are brothers, no more and no less. 'You have only one Master and you are all brothers' (Matthew 23:8). The divisive and artificial categories of clergy and laity are not only *un*scriptural, they are *anti*-scriptural, militating against the fundamental spirit of the New Testament.

Even the all-time greats of the early church bore no special titles. James, the leader of the church in Jerusalem, is just James (Galatians 2:12); Peter is referred to as Peter (1 Corinthians 15:5 etc.) or as Cephas (1 Corinthians 9:5 etc.), while the great apostle to the Gentiles is simply 'our dear brother Paul' (2 Peter 3:15).

There is no biblical reason why *any* believer in Christ should not dispense the bread and wine. At the Passover it was the father who presided, as head of the family, but it would be an unwarranted deduction to conclude from that that only a leader of the church should preside at the Lord's Supper. That would in any case curtail its celebration in homes or in small groups with no elder present.

In fact, we would do well to ditch the word 'preside', which is lacking in biblical precedent and rich in ritual overtones foreign to the New Testament. Paul talks about 'the cup . . . for which *we* give thanks' (1 Corinthians 10:16). His use of 'we' suggests that any believer may give thanks for it as a preliminary to passing it round.

Giving thanks

Notice, too, that we 'give thanks' for it. The notion of 'consecration' of the bread and wine is absent. Perhaps it grew out of Paul's use of the Greek word *eulogeo* (meaning 'to bless') and its variants in 1 Corinthians 10:16, just quoted. The King James Version translates it, 'The cup of blessing which we bless . . . .' All modern translations render it, more correctly, 'The cup of thanksgiving for which we give thanks.'

Let a biblical scholar explain: 'The cup of blessing was a Jewish technical term for the cup of wine for which a blessing, i.e. thanksgiving, was given to God. The idea that the cup was blessed, rather than God, is one that dies hard and has been used to justify some kind of "consecration" of the elements in modern liturgies whereby they become vehicles of divine blessing to those who receive them. But 1 Corinthians 14:16 shows that by "bless" Paul meant the giving of thanks to God, and this fits in with the Jewish practice of blessing God for his gifts of food and drink.'[5]

The giving of thanks is something that *every* Christian is not only equipped but enjoined to do (1 Thessalonians 5:18). There is no reason at all, therefore, why he or she should not give thanks for the bread and wine.

Having said that, the giving of thanks in this context should not be viewed slavishly, as if the bread and wine were somehow not properly prepared for consumption without this formality.

I recall one occasion when someone began to pass the bread round as we were bowed before God in a time of silent adoration. One man, noticing this, sprang to his feet with 'We haven't given thanks for it', and proceeded to do so in a way which was both dull and foreign to the atmosphere of the moment. Tradition can be grossly indelicate!

At domestic meals, sometimes we say grace and sometimes we don't; grace (in both senses) suffers when it becomes a legalistic practice. The same holds good at the Lord's Supper. The main thing at both is that our hearts be full of thanks to the Lord.

We conclude, then, that the celebration of the meal should be often rather than seldom; that we should prefer normal bread served on an ordinary plate and wine in an everyday glass; that any genuine believer may dispense them; and that the giving of thanks beforehand is desirable, though not obligatory.

Now we must consider the broader question of the general atmosphere in which the Lord's Supper should take place.

Chapter 11 NOTES

1. D. Bridge & D. Phypers, *The Meal that Unites?* Hodder & Stoughton, 1981, p24
2. W. Barclay, *The Lord's Supper,* SCM Press, 1967, p107
3. I.H. Marshall, *Last Supper and Lord's Supper,* Paternoster Press, 1980, p149
4. P. Dixon, *The Truth About AIDS,* Kingsway Publications, 1987, p97
5. Marshall, p120

12

How to
eat supper

Poker-faced ritual and stuffy religiosity aren't God's style. In all his dealings with us, he is delightfully down-to-earth.

He talked to Noah in a shipyard, to Gideon in a wine-press and to Balaam by means of a donkey. He had Moses scrabbling up a mountain, to arrive for his rendezvous with the Almighty puffing, sweaty and red in the face. The tabernacle, in plain language, was a mere tent, and the ark of the covenant, for all its tremendous significance, had two poles attached so that it could be carried around on men's shoulders!

God's ordinances have always been earthy, too, and in most cases downright messy. The site of the Levitical offerings was a religious abattoir. Circumcision focused attention on a boy-child's most private part, to the accompaniment of his screams. As for baptism — the biblical kind, by immersion — it's hard to be serious in the face of the spluttering, gasping and eye-rubbing that mingle with the hallelujahs as the candidate rises from the water.

We could say the same about meals. Ritual formality is ill at ease at a proper meal where, in spite of attention to manners, there is chewing, swallowing, sipping, gulping (not to mention burping), drips down one's front and crumbs on the floor.

God's presence and power, it seems, prefer to reside in

these everyday situations of humankind. Didn't Jesus —
God's presence and power incarnate — make his entry in
a tatty shed behind an inn?

Holy informality

Informality is important. Acceptance of its place in God's
dealings with us must be our starting point in considering
some of the mechanics of celebrating the Lord's Supper.

The sober sipping of a thimbleful of wine and attempts
to chew a morsel of bread 'spiritually', without moving the
jaw, remain a world apart from real eating and drinking.
Readers from a ritualistic background, therefore, must make
a huge effort to rid themselves of attitudes ingrained by
centuries of off-centre church history. They must embrace
the earthiness of true spirituality.

Informality, be assured, is not disorder. Paul's prescription
of 'everything . . . done in a fitting and orderly way' (1
Corinthians 14:40) holds good for us as it did for the
Corinthians.

By informality I mean the refusal to put on a special
religious manner for certain activities. 'Now let us begin the
meeting proper by singing hymn number . . .' — that's a
religious manner. So is the pseudo-pious facial expression
reminiscent of an El Greco portrait, and the feeling that it
would be irreverent to blow one's nose before the service ends.

New Testament Christianity was *real*. The people were
naturally supernatural. It's hard to imagine a meeting starting
promptly at eleven o'clock and finishing by twelve. In Acts
20, a meeting which included the Lord's Supper went on
all night, with guest speaker Paul 'talking until daylight' (v11).
The word 'talking' means 'conversing' — people chipped in
with questions and comments, like real people do.

In Jerusalem, the Christians broke bread 'in their homes
. . . with glad and sincere hearts' (Acts 2:46). Gladness and
formality are uncomfortable bedfellows, whereas gladness and
sincerity are truly compatible, especially in the relaxed
atmosphere of a home.

When did you last celebrate the Lord's Supper in an ordinary house? It's an ideal setting. The Passover was a house-based celebration (Exodus 12:7), and Jesus ate the Last Supper in some householder's upper room. Both of these were *real* meals, however, not just symbolic ones. Informality is easier in a real-meal atmosphere. Should we then return to combining the two?

This brings us back to the *agapé* or love-feast, with which the Lord's Supper used to be combined. The Jerusalem Christians 'broke bread in their homes (the Lord's Supper) and ate together (the fellowship meal)' (Acts 2:46). Where the Corinthians met isn't clear — possibly a large house belonging to one of the wealthier members — but they certainly combined the *agapé* with the Lord's Supper (1 Corinthians 11).

But even at this early stage there were signs that Paul wanted to play down the real-meal aspects, probably in view of the wild abuse as well as the organisational problems of a large crowd's eating together. 'Don't you have homes to eat and drink in?' he asks (v22), adding, 'If anyone is hungry, he should eat at home' (v34).

Flexible gatherings

This raises the question of numbers in the church. We don't know how many believers there were at Corinth when Paul wrote his letters. We *do* know that in Jerusalem there were many thousands (Acts 2:41, 47; 4:4) and, since the messengers of the gospel were accused by pagans of turning the world upside down (Acts 17:6), it is reasonable to suppose that other major cities had similar numbers.

Where, then, did they meet? Seeing themselves at first as a Jewish sect, the Jerusalem Christians 'continued to meet together in the temple courts', but they 'broke bread in their homes' (Acts 2:46). Clearly they were flexible. In Exodus 12 the same flexibility is evident: the Passover is presented as relevant to 'all the people of the community of Israel' (verses 6, 19, 47), but also to each 'family' or 'household' (v3 etc.) and even to 'each person' (v4).

We should be flexible, too. Special buildings enabling churches numbering several thousand to assemble are a useful asset. But since Christianity has no holy places, only holy people, believers loyal to a common eldership may legitimately meet in smaller congregations, from a regional gathering of, say, two hundred in a school hall to a house-size group of twenty-five or even half a dozen. It is still a meeting of the church, because the church is people.

Arranging bread and wine for thousands presents logistical problems, though it may well be worth the effort from time to time. But everything points to the wisdom of celebrating the Lord's Supper chiefly in smaller and more intimate settings, whether combined with a meal or not. At the Last Supper there were just Jesus and the Twelve — an ideal number, perhaps?

My wife and I often have Christian friends round for an evening meal. After eating, we relax over coffee and chat — about matters both trivial and serious. Sometimes, before our guests leave, I will bring in from the kitchen a slice of bread and the wine remaining from our meal. These we will share, with prayer and a warm embrace, reminding ourselves of the wonderful togetherness we enjoy in Christ. It takes only two or three minutes, but it is the Lord's Supper, and very precious.

Occasionally, as the head of the house, I will do the same just with my wife and children, all of whom love the Lord. We are part of the church, a covenant family; it is right for us to share the covenant meal.

In the history of the church, even after the *agapé* and the Lord's Supper had become separated, the *agapé* continued as a feature of church life for several centuries. It is a feature worth reviving. But whether we combine it with the Lord's Supper or not, let's be sure to continue taking the bread and wine in a meal-like atmosphere of holy informality.

13

Being real

As a rule, it is in informal settings that we are truly ourselves. I recall seeing a farmer sitting soberly in a Methodist chapel, dutifully singing the hymns, listening to the sermon and adding his formal amens to the prayers. Outside at the end of the service, I saw the same man sucking on his pipe and, in the company of one or two other men, verbally tearing the minister to shreds.

Which was the true man? The one outside. Informality had removed his mask. Somehow, a formal setting makes it easier to be hypocritical; the formality provides a handy cloak for covering unworthy motives and attitudes. Since formality in church meetings is widespread, it is hardly surprising that, in the common opinion, Christians are a bunch of hypocrites.

Hypocrisy means putting on an act, wearing a mask, giving an impression other than the truth. By that definition, many professing Christians are hypocrites indeed, and nowhere does their hypocrisy show up more clearly than in this 'duty' of going to church, often practised in the belief that their giving to God of one hour per week will make them more acceptable in his sight.

Churchgoing as a mere appendage to normal life, however, is not a biblical practice. Acting one way inside supposedly holy walls and another way outside of them is hypocrisy based upon error, for no church building may legitimately be called

'the house of God'. The house of God is people, not buildings
— not even ones bedecked with all the soulish trappings of
ecclesiasticism such as spires, stained glass, altars and the
like (Hebrews 3:6; 2 Corinthians 6:16; Ephesians 2:21; 1
Peter 2:5).

The church, as we have already observed, is not where we
go, it is *what we are*. It is believers in Jesus living the spiritual
life twenty-four hours a day. So when Christians meet
together in a building which we traditionally call a church,
they should not act any differently from the way they would
act outside. If we laugh outside, why shouldn't we laugh
inside? — assuming, that is, that the circumstances call for
laughter.

Spiritual schizophrenia

The practice of churchgoing has bred in many people a kind
of spiritual schizophrenia. As soon as they enter the church
or chapel premises, they abandon normality and put on their
church masks — especially if they have no contact with each
other outside of such places. They slip into what has been
called 'back of the neck Christianity' — the practice of sitting
in a pew for an hour, looking at the back of someone's neck
and going through certain religious routines.

The service over, they exit from the building, remove their
masks and, like the farmer, return to normality.

I hasten to add that not all who attend Christian meetings
of the traditional kind are like this. Praise God for all those
true believers in Jesus, filled with the Holy Spirit, who are
to be found in every kind of church setting, from Roman
Catholic to Quaker.

But if the local church is essentially what we are rather
than where we go, our times together for worship, including
the Lord's Supper, will simply be extensions of the life we
share the rest of the time. If Jesus is, as he must be, part
and parcel of normal living, there is no need to put on a mask
when we assemble to remember him more specifically in the
Lord's Supper.

In other words, a hallmark of the covenant community will always be *reality*. We will be as free to laugh, weep, comment, shout, applaud and jump up and down in church meetings as we are at the football match. We will also be as free to sit in thoughtful silence in church meetings as we are when watching a TV documentary on third world famine at home.

Normality of life and behaviour in church meetings extends to the Lord's Supper. Remembering the Lord in the breaking of bread will be an occasion for reality in our dealings with one another.

Speaking the truth in love

In particular, it will be an opportunity for *frank speaking*. Nothing is more down to earth than a family round a meal table. Knowing each other the way they do, they have long since given up projecting images, putting on airs and trying to live on a diet of polite small-talk. In the covenant community of the local church, the Lord's Supper is a family gathering, an extended opportunity for that 'speaking the truth in love' which marks the members' life in general.

Jesus always spoke frankly and truthfully to his disciples, and he didn't stop at the Last Supper. The fact that it was an important ceremonial occasion in Jewish life didn't stop it being a place for relaxed and normal conversation. Some of the truths spoken were unpalatable: 'While they were reclining at the table eating, he said, "I tell you the truth, one of you will betray me"' (Mark 14:18). Again, 'You are clean, though not every one of you' (John 13:10). And Jesus didn't beat around the bush; when Judas said, 'Surely not I, Rabbi?' his reply was, 'Yes, it is you' (Matthew 26:25-26).

Sincere and truthful talk comes out of sincere and truthful hearts. We are to 'keep the Festival . . . with . . . the bread of sincerity and truth' (1 Corinthians 5:8), like the early believers who 'broke bread in their homes and ate together with glad and sincere hearts' (Acts 2:46).

Oh for an injection of sincerity and truth into the false piety of much present-day Christianity! But not until local churches begin to live as covenant communities can they ever hope to enjoy frank speaking round the meal table.

Encouragement at Supper

One way in which that frankness will find expression is in *mutual encouragement*. True covenant love believes the best. It looks for little tokens of growth and progress and hails them as milestones of personal pilgrimage. What a joy to share bread and wine with a brother and, looking him in the eye, say, 'John, you've come a long way in the last few months, you know. That old edginess has gone; you're so much more relaxed.'

'Do you really think so, Dave?'

'Yes, I do.'

'That's fantastic! I've really been working on it — with the Lord's help, of course. But I don't know, sometimes the progress seems awfully slow. It's great that you noticed.'

'Well, I did. And I'm not the only one. A couple of other folk have commented on it as well, so be encouraged — you really have changed!'

John's eyes fill up. We each tear off a piece of bread and eat it together, followed by a mouthful of wine. We join in a brotherly embrace and I pray for him: 'Lord, thank you for this brother of mine. You've done a wonderful job in him by your Spirit. Thank you for the obvious progress I can see in his life. Thank you for the new level of rest and peace in his whole manner. Lord, please continue the work you've begun. Amen.'

'God, you're just so wonderful! I'd never have changed at all without your help,' prays John, fighting hard to keep control of his voice. 'Thank you, Lord, for everything. I love you. And thanks for Dave and his encouragement today. Wow, Lord, it really is fantastic when brothers dwell together in unity this way!'

When did you last come away from the Lord's Supper with your shoulder wet from someone else's tears?

If Jesus was an inveterate encourager of his family of

disciples, we must learn from him. And he *was* an encourager. Knowing what lay just ahead of the Last Supper, he could have been heavily critical of that slow-minded, stubborn bunch who would soon desert him. But no. 'You,' he said, 'are those who have stood by me in my trials. And I confer on you a kingdom . . . so that you may eat and drink at my table in my kingdom' (Luke 22:28-30).

Paul took a similar approach. 'Nobody should seek his own good, but the good of others,' he counselled in the context of his teaching on the Lord's Supper (1 Corinthians 10:24). We couldn't blame him if, in view of the appalling excesses of behaviour in the Corinthian church, he had had nothing to express but disapproval. But instead, he urged them to be godly, kind and holy, *'as you really are'* (1 Corinthians 5:7). What an encourager he was!

In the holy informality of the Lord's Supper we have a prime opportunity to speak the truth to each other and offer mutual encouragement. Let's do it, then, even if we do get dubbed 'the wet shoulder brigade'!

14

Looking back, looking up

Once we are clear about who should be included on the Lord's Supper guest-list and how they should conduct themselves, we can focus our attention on the *significance* of the covenant meal. And what is that?

Remembrance

To begin with, it is an occasion for looking back — a time for *remembrance*.

When all who partake are the redeemed of the Lord, they can look back to Christ's death with real feeling, because each of them has a personal stake in it. The roots of our salvation lie in the cross of Christ. 'Whenever you eat this bread and drink this cup,' says Paul, 'you proclaim *the Lord's death*' (1 Corinthians 11:26).

We have already noted the memorial aspects of the Passover. The people looked back to a lamb killed, to blood applied, and remembered the agonising cries of the Egyptians at the death of the firstborn. Death brushed even their own doors, but could not enter: 'When I see the blood, I will pass over you.'

The covenant, too, had been sealed in blood. Their minds went back to that awesome moment when the people of Israel had assembled near Sinai for the public reading of the Book of the Covenant. They remembered their united cry: 'We

will do everything the Lord has said; we will obey.' Then
Moses had come among them, sprinkling the sacrificial blood,
and they had peered down at the stains as it spattered on
their garments while Moses' voice proclaimed, 'This is the
blood of the covenant'.

That blood, that animal's death, had bound them in a
solemn agreement which, far from being momentary,
produced a lasting effect upon their whole lifestyle: it bound
them to the keeping of God's law on pain of death. That
past event had present implications.

So it is with the Lord's Supper. All our present freedoms
and privileges can be traced back to an historical event —
a man hanging on a Roman cross on a hill outside Jerusalem.
His death saw the shedding of the blood of the new covenant,
a covenant by which we are joyfully bound, not to
burdensome legal obligations but to new life in the Spirit
and all the blessings of a people who live under 'a better
covenant' (Hebrews 7:22).

It is proper that we should look back. But not in a mournful
manner. The Lord's Supper was never meant to be a funeral
supper, because Jesus didn't stay dead for long. He burst
out of death's grip into glorious resurrection life, and he's
alive today!

Rejoicing

Running parallel to our looking *back* to the cross, therefore,
must be a looking *up* to 'where Christ is seated at the right
hand of God' (Colossians 3:1). As well as being a time for
remembrance, the Lord's Supper is a time for *rejoicing!*

The bread and wine are not funeral fare. Jesus didn't say,
'Do this in remembrance of my death'; he said, 'Do this in
remembrance of *me,* ' — that is, 'of all that I am to you' —
and it is a risen, glorified Lord Jesus that we bring to mind
in the Supper.

I recall the Christian who, eagerly witnessing to a non-
Christian friend, enthused, 'Jesus isn't dead, he's alive!'

'How do you know?'

'I was talking to him this morning!'

When Jesus is such a living reality to us, there's no way we can get bogged down in the graveyard syndrome of hushed voices, plaintive melodies and dirge-like hymns about the gory details of the cross. To remember Christ's death is immediately to be forced on to his rising, to his triumphant ascension and our living relationship with him today.

Here is where many protestant Christians have gone wrong. In reacting against the idea of transubstantiation — of a Christ physically present here and now in the bread and wine — they have reduced the Lord's Supper to a mere memorial — a backwards look to the cross and no more. This was Zwingli's view, born of overreaction, at the time of the Reformation.

A mere memorial can produce, at best, only sadness. In one sense, of course, a mere memorial is an impossibility. As Broughton Knox puts it: 'No spiritually minded believer can remember the Lord without at the same time being in conscious fellowship with him through the Spirit, so that a 'bare remembrance' is impossible, while genuine remembrance is fellowship with Christ, than which no higher blessing is possible.'[1]

Certainly we search the New Testament in vain for any associations of sorrow with the Lord's Supper. These seem to have crept in at a later stage, when the whole thing was in a state of deterioration.

Howard Marshall concludes: 'The New Testament does not appear to associate sorrow or mourning over the death of Jesus with the celebration of the Supper. The Supper was not an occasion for mourning over his death, but rather for rejoicing in his presence and giving thanks for the benefits procured by his death. Whatever may have happened in a later period, the early church remembered at the Supper what the Lord's death had provided rather than grieved over the fact that he had to die.'[2]

Resurrection is the New Testament's emphasis. 'Since Christ was raised from the dead, he cannot die again' (Romans

6:9). The first day of the week is resurrection day, not death day, and our celebration of the Supper (whether it takes place on that day or another) is a celebration of *life!* Whenever I break bread with my brothers and sisters, amid much thanksgiving, embracing and mutual prayer, my eyes nearly always grow moist, not with sadness but with the sheer wonder of our common life in Jesus. He is alive in us and among us; our mutual covenant love is the living proof of it.

Perhaps we should see in the term 'the Lord's Supper' a suggestion that the living Lord Jesus is the host. It is *his* supper, to which he welcomes us as guests. 'Where two or three come together in my name, there am I with them' (Matthew 18:20).

At the Lord's Supper, hope is restored, flagging spirits are revived, new life and vigour are injected into the body of Christ. We experience a replay of the events on the Emmaus road, where those two disciples were trudging the seven miles from Jerusalem to Emmaus, weary, downcast and dispirited. The newly-risen Jesus met up with them and 'was recognised by them when he broke the bread' (Luke 24:35).

Suddenly, both the physical weariness and the spiritual depression were gone. The two disciples thought nothing of footing it the seven miles back to Jerusalem to blurt out to their fellows the details of their encounter with the living Christ: 'He's alive! He's alive — and we've met him!'

All meals are meant to be happy occasions, and none more so than this covenant meal. Here we encounter the living Christ and here we are refreshed in both body and spirit. Here we declare to one another, 'He's alive!'

Strengthened to give thanks

Like the original Passover meal, which fortified the Israelites for the long march to the promised land, the Lord's Supper provides us with strength for the spiritual journey ahead of us. It is hard to imagine those Israelites pondering long on the slaughter of the lamb. Their remembrance was swiftly overtaken by the excitement of the exodus: the new nation, fortified by a stomach full of roast lamb, was on its way to God's appointed destination. They felt ready for anything!

It's the same with us. We rightly recall the slaughter of Calvary, but 'Christ in us, the hope of glory' quickly turns our attention to the exciting realities of our present pilgrimage. Like a meal at a wayside inn, the Supper strengthens our faith for the rest of the journey. At that meal, we sit with the sparkle of faith in our eyes to eat Christ's flesh and drink his blood in the sense of John 6 — reaffirming our faith in him.

We take the 'cup of thanksgiving', therefore, not in a solemn liturgical ritual but in joyful recognition of the boundless grace of God towards us in Christ Jesus. It is 'a participation in the blood of Christ' (1 Corinthians 10:16), a concrete reminder that — glory to God! — we have a stake in the new covenant privileges and blessings which were signed over to the people of God by the covenant blood of Jesus.

When a 'Hallelujah!' rises to our lips, therefore, we don't swallow it back down with the wine — we let it out!

Most modern translations of 1 Corinthians 10:16 render Paul's words thus: 'the cup of thanksgiving for which we give thanks . . . .' Perhaps Coverdale had a point when, in his 1535 translation, he gave it a different, and quite legitimate, slant: 'the cup of thanksgiving *with* which we give thanks.'

We are to be a people marked out by our endless thanksgiving. Unlike unbelievers who, 'although they knew God . . . neither glorified him as God nor gave thanks to him' (Romans 1:21), we rejoice in the Lord *always* and *in everything* give thanks (Philippians 4:4; 1 Thessalonians 5:18). We do so when times are hard as well as when they are easy, just as Jesus at the Last Supper handed out the bread 'when he had given thanks' (1 Corinthians 11:24), in spite of the dark shadow of the approaching cross.

Let's then come to the table with joyful hearts. Away with that pious formality which is incompatible with genuine thanksgiving. No more of the funereal solemnity which religious tradition has thrust upon us.

In Forsyth's words, 'Let us get rid of the idea which has impoverished worship beyond measure, that the act is mainly commemorative. No church can live on that. How can we have a mere memorial of one who is still alive, still our life, still present with us and acting in us?'[3]

Chapter 14 NOTES

1. D.B. Knox, *The Lord's Supper from Wycliffe to Cranmer,* Paternoster Press, 1983, p65
2. I.H. Marshall, *Last Supper and Lord's Supper,* Paternoster Press, 1980, p153
3. P.T. Forsyth, *The Church and the Sacraments,* Longmans, Green & Co., 1917, p215

15

Heightened reality

The rejoicing of the last chapter can take a knock when we read Paul's puzzling and alarming statements about judgment at the Lord's Supper (1 Corinthians 11:28-30).

Weakness, sickness and death, it seems, had fallen upon some of the Corinthian Christians because of their unworthy participation in the Supper. We know that a holy God must punish sin, but why, we naturally wonder, should they be judged by God for their behaviour at the covenant meal in particular rather than for their behaviour in general?

To answer that question we must refresh our minds about the meaning of meals. A meal, we observed earlier, is a time for *togetherness*. This aspect is highlighted by the New Testament's use, in describing the Lord's Supper, of the Greek word *deipnon*. The *deipnon* was the main meal of the day in Bible times, taken in the evening when the members of a family came together to eat after their separate daytime pursuits.

A meal is also *an occasion*, a special time for focusing on our friendship with family, friends and guests over food and drink.

We noticed, too, how in Bible times a meal was often more than that. It had religious overtones. In many contexts it became *a sacred act uniting the eaters*.

Recalling the criticism levelled by the Pharisees against

Jesus for his eating with tax collectors and sinners, we noticed that the meal table was *a place of association*. By eating with a certain man you indicated your acceptance of him and your loyalty to him. 'The table at which you eat is the loyalty to which you are pledged.'[1]

Then we considered, in particular, covenant meals, which placed *obligations upon the participants in terms of their relationship with each other*. To repeat the meal, the way Jews kept the Passover meal each year, was to renew their covenant commitments, first to the Lord and then to one another.

Barclay illustrates all these implications in his explanation of David's famous sentence, 'You prepare a table before me in the presence of my enemies' (Psalm 23:5):

> The picture is that of a man fleeing across the desert with his enemies hot on his heels. He arrives at an encampment where the family are at a meal. He stands before the open tent in hesitation and in mute appeal. If the man in the tent stretches out his hand and offers him food, bread and salt, he is safe, for he will be accepted into the encampment and, if need be, defended to the last. But if the man in the tent turns away and refuses, the fugitive is left to face his enemies alone. The giving and the sharing of the meal is the mark of committed friendship. Those who sit at a meal are committed to each other, and committed to their host, and their host is committed to them.'[2]

At the Lord's Supper, Jesus himself is the host. He saw us as spiritual fugitives and stretched out his hand in welcome. Now we find ourselves seated at his table with other ex-fugitives, and in sharing the meal with them we express our commitment not only to our host, Jesus, but to our fellow-eaters. We are bound by covenant, vertically and horizontally.

A sharpening of focus

The key to understanding why God's judgment is drawn towards the Lord's Supper as lightning is drawn towards a tower lies in these observations about meals.

The point is that, because of everything that eating together signifies, *the everyday realities of the new covenant are heightened when we share the covenant meal.* They are brought into sharper focus. Their deep significance is highlighted. The rewards of covenant faithfulness become more apparent, and the penalties of neglect strike home with greater force.

By way of illustration, imagine a woman who is becoming frustrated with her husband. In a moment of deep sadness and anger she shouts over her shoulder, 'I don't love you any more!' The man is devastated. She can't possibly mean it, can she? Surely it was just a statement thrown out in the heat of the moment as she stalked out of the door. Or was it?

He must know. So he follows her through to the other room, turns her round to face him and says, 'Can you look me in the eye and say that again?'

As she meets his gaze and the windows of their souls are opened to one another, she finds the words sticking in her throat. In the heightened awareness of the eyeball-to-eyeball situation, words which before slipped out easily are now subjected to a more stringent test of reality.

Take another case. Graham has always prided himself on being straightforward and truthful. He would be hard-pressed to tell a lie. Today he is in court, a witness in an important case. As he mounts the witness box he takes the oath, promising before God to tell 'the truth, the whole truth and nothing but the truth'.

Suddenly, he has a heightened awareness of the importance of telling the truth. Truthfulness has always been Graham's practice, but in this special situation, it assumes a vivid new importance. Life imposes its own penalties when we tell lies, but the penalties for perjury — for lying under oath — are altogether more serious.

This is exactly the kind of heightened spiritual reality that marks our participation in the covenant meal of the Lord's Supper. Hopefully, we live as a covenant community all the time, but at the Supper we are eyeball-to-eyeball, so to speak, telling each other in the meal, 'I love you.' We are 'under oath' before God and each other.

Numbers 5 provides a biblical illustration. A woman suspected of adultery would be taken to the priest and invited 'under oath' (v19) to drink the 'water of jealousy', a beverage which, under God, would reveal her true moral position. If she was innocent it would do her no harm. In fact, it would do her good, because she would be justified before her husband and fellow-citizens and be able to live her life with a new dignity. But if she was guilty, the drinking of the 'water that brings a curse' would cause her 'thigh to waste away' and her 'abdomen to swell' (v21-22). She would suffer physically (by being unable to bear children) and be branded an adulteress.

The drinking of water is in itself an everyday occurrence. The water was ordinary (as indeed are the bread and wine of communion), but this was no ordinary drinking — it had spiritual significance. In the providence of God, it was calculated to find her out, either for good or for ill.

The case of Judas

In the New Testament, Judas is a case in point. A meal found him out, too.

John records that when the Passover meal was being served, 'the devil had already prompted Judas Iscariot, son of Simon, to betray Jesus' (John 13:2). Judas sat down to chew over the commitment-food with his teeth and betrayal with his mind. What a dangerous discrepancy! His willingness to share in the meal with Jesus proclaimed, 'I'm with you and for you,' while in his heart he was saying, 'I'm against you.'

During the meal, Jesus made it known that one of them would betray him, the one to whom he would give the sop, or piece of dipped bread. 'Then,' John continues, 'dipping the piece of bread, he gave it to Judas Iscariot, son of Simon. *As soon as Judas took the bread, Satan entered into him*' (John 13:26-27).

Notice how the sharing of the meal, especially his acceptance from Jesus of the bread, crystallised the state of Judas's heart. Satan, who before had been content to prompt, now took over. What had begun in Judas's heart as a mere inclination towards betrayal now became a fixation. It was the meal that did it.

The covenant meal is a dangerous place for hypocrites. Though his heart had harboured thoughts of betrayal, Judas had gone through all the normal motions of friendship, secure (or so he had thought) in the knowledge that no-one was aware of his evil intentions. So when all the others had said, 'Surely not I, Lord?' (Matthew 26:22), he had had the audacity to say the same.

He was still playing the same game at Jesus' arrest, when he greeted him in the customary way with the word 'Rabbi!' and a kiss. But it was too late. The meal had already found him out.

This is the tragedy of Judas, and it could be the tragedy today of those who eat the Lord's Supper with betrayal, or some other unworthy attitude, in their hearts. The meal signifies togetherness, commitment, harmony and mutual love. To eat that meal with contrary heart-attitudes of rebellion, self-seeking, disharmony or betrayal is to court disaster. Those who shout 'Yes' when they really mean 'No' are guilty of spiritual perjury and are ripe for judgment.

It is this fearful incompatibility — eating the covenant meal with a heart full of anti-covenant hatred — which lends force to the statements of Jesus, 'The one who has *dipped his hand into the bowl with me* will betray me' (Matthew 26:23) and, 'One of you will betray me — *one who is eating with me*' (Mark 14:18). He quotes the Psalmist: 'He who *shares my bread* has lifted up his heel against me' (John 13:18).

And again: 'It is *one of the Twelve*' (Mark 14:20) — one of that committed inner circle who shared meals together. Mark records Jesus as saying, 'Here comes my betrayer!' adding, 'Just as he was speaking, Judas, *one of the Twelve*, appeared' (Mark 14:42-43). It is an awful thing to be reckoned as part of the committed group and go through the motions of commitment when the heart is set on betrayal.

More than any other facet of Christian fellowship in

general, and of the Lord's Supper in particular, it is this one which today's covenant community — the church of Christ — desperately needs to understand.

A two-edged sword

The sobering fact is that, because God himself has built into the Lord's Supper this principle of heightened reality, it continues to operate even when we ourselves remain ignorant of it or forget it.

The Christians in Corinth appear to have been ignorant of it. Or they had forgotten, perhaps, that the Word of God is a two-edged sword, bringing both blessings and curses, depending on our attitude. By sharing the bread and wine they were proclaiming their oneness in Christ — their covenant unity — while at the same time the church was split from top to bottom by factions and gross selfishness.

'That is why many among you are weak and sick,' Paul concludes, 'and a number of you have fallen asleep' — in other words, have died prematurely (1 Corinthians 11:30). Their ignorance or forgetfulness, whichever it was, clearly had done nothing to shield them from God's judgment.

Some have argued that we live in a different age from them, with different values, and that therefore we can't expect the same blessings (for sincerity) and penalties (for duplicity) to apply to us.

For one who makes such a strong appeal to the New Testament, it is astonishing to see Howard Marshall taking such a view. He comments: 'Paul interprets these calamities as judgments upon sin. It is, therefore, Paul's *interpretation* of these events which raises questions. All that we can say is that he believed that divine judgment could overtake those who participated unworthily in the sacrament; it is not a view that is generally shared in modern Western Christendom which holds that, whatever may have happened in the first century, this kind of connection cannot be drawn today.'[3]

But the connection can and, I am convinced, must be drawn. Of course, some professing Christians, many of them unregenerate, will remain content to go through the motions of bread-eating and wine-drinking in ritualistic church services. They have no desire for the seven-days-a-week living oneness that the meal implies. Those, for example, who cringe even at the 'sign of peace' — an optional handshake or similar greeting during the Anglican communion service — will have no time for the deeper togetherness of life and worship that marks a true covenant community.

Just as some go through a form of baptism and, being unregenerate, come out unchanged except for being wet, these will 'take communion' and leave unchanged except for the few grams of bread and wine in their stomachs. Their eating and drinking is so far removed from Christ's intention that it is hard to see them coming under divine judgment for it. Their participation isn't evil; it's just irrelevant — and should be discouraged for that very reason.

But right across the denominations today there are men, women and children, truly the Lord's, with a deep hunger for more reality — in their personal walk with God and in their church life. It is a worthy desire.

Yet they must realise that to draw near to a covenant-keeping God, especially in the breaking of bread, has double implications. It brings his covenant blessings closer: love, strength, healing and provision come within reach in a whole new way. But the covenant penalties come closer, too: we can't share in the covenant meal in sinful disregard of our fellow-believers and get away with it.

Chapter 15 NOTES

1. E.F. Kevan, *The Lord's Supper,* Evangelical Press, 1966, p46
2. W. Barclay, *The Lord's Supper,* SCM Press, 1967, p45
3. I.H. Marshall, *Last Supper and Lord's Supper,* Paternoster Press, 1980, p115

Divine judgment and self-examination

God is a Judge. True, he is a loving Father to his children, but he is still a Judge, his very nature requiring him to draw a line between good and evil, between the acceptable and the unacceptable.

The final expression of his judgment will be at the end, of course, 'when he will judge the world with justice by the man he has appointed' (Acts 17:31). But he remains a Judge in the meantime, too. We can no more separate God's judgment from himself than we can separate the sunlight from the sun. He is a Judge *now*.

And what has this to do with the Lord's Supper? A great deal, for the covenant meal is a place of judgment. We have seen how, at that meal, the realities of our relationship with God and with each other are brought into sharper focus. Since judgment is one of those realities, it too becomes heightened at the covenant meal.

The Passover, out of which that meal was born, took place in the very midst of judgment: 'I will bring judgment on all the gods of Egypt. I am the Lord' (Exodus 11:12). Sheltered by the shed blood, the people of Israel remained safe. But once on their way to the promised land as the holy nation, they quickly realised that the judgment of God which had devastated Egypt could just as readily descend upon themselves, the covenant people, if they fell short of their covenant obligations.

In fact, God dealt with them more strictly than with anyone else. And why not? That's the way fathers normally deal with their children.

Father and family

Sometimes, when my children were young, their friends would come to play and things would get out of hand. A window would be broken or a curtain pulled down. And with whom did I deal the more strictly — with my own children or with their friends? With my own, of course. Their friends would be told curtly, 'Go home now,' then I would show my children that being a loving father was compatible with being a judge!

It is *because* they were my children that I would take their misdemeanours seriously. In fact, my judgment was an expression of my love for them, of my concern that they should grow up with sound values, social graces and good character.

God is like that. 'It is time,' says Peter, 'for judgment to *begin with the family of God*' (1 Peter 4:17). That's why judgment has a proper place at the Lord's Supper — the family meal.

We could say that God will not tolerate bad table manners. And at Corinth the table manners were appalling: 'When you come together,' Paul complains, 'it is not the Lord's Supper you eat, for as you eat, each of you goes ahead without waiting for anybody else. One remains hungry, another gets drunk.'

Then he proceeds to instruct them in better behaviour, 'so that when you meet together it may not result in judgment' (1 Corinthians 11:20-21, 34).

In chapter ten we saw how the Corinthian church members in general and their leaders in particular had to be responsible for the church's purity, refusing to admit unbelievers as part of the committed body and judging sin among the Christians. They were to clear out 'the yeast of malice and wickedness' from the house of God just as Jews used to go through their houses and throw out any remaining yeast before the Passover.

But there is also a personal aspect to the judgment which God requires of us. 'Whoever eats the bread or drinks the cup of the Lord in an unworthy manner will be guilty of sinning against the body and blood of the Lord,' Paul points out. Therefore, he continues, 'a man ought to examine *himself* before he eats of the bread and drinks of the cup' (1 Corinthians 11:27-28). Why? Because by exercising proper *self*-judgment, he will avoid the judgment of God (v31).

The worm mentality

What does self-examination mean? We can say at once what it doesn't mean: it doesn't mean saying to myself, 'I'm a wretched sinner, utterly unworthy of the love of God. Therefore I'll humbly sit back and let the bread and wine pass by, lest by taking them I call down God's judgment upon myself.'

Of course I'm unworthy! So are we all. But the glory of the gospel is that Jesus Christ is worthy and that his worthiness has been put to our account as a gift of his grace. Having received 'God's abundant provision of grace and of the gift of righteousness' (Romans 5:17), we stand worthy before God and can therefore come worthily to the Supper.

The worm mentality is one of the great curses of the celebration of the covenant meal in most traditional circles. Beaten over the head with the Ten Commandments, people come to the table convinced more than ever that they are miserable sinners. One writer puts it this way: 'To be burdened with your sin, even to be weighed down with a sense of your guilt and utter unworthiness — that is to take the Lord's Supper worthily.'[1]

What nonsense! 'There is now *no condemnation* for those who are in Christ Jesus' (Romans 8:1). How can we come cringing into God's presence when, 'since we have been justified by faith, we have peace with God through our Lord

Jesus Christ' (Romans 5:1)? Far from cringing, we may 'approach the throne of grace with confidence' (Hebrews 4:16). Certainly, we respect the Ten Commandments as the expression of God's will for us, but we remember that 'by dying to what once bound us, we have been released from the law so that we serve in the new way of the Spirit, and not in the old way of the written code' (Romans 7:6).

At this point some will throw up their hands and cry 'Antinomian!', protesting that I am confusing justification and sanctification, our righteous standing before God and our present imperfect state of holiness.

But no, I understand the difference very well. I appreciate what has been called 'the standing paradox of sanctification' — that the more Christlike we become, the more we realise remains in us still to be conformed to his image. But that realisation, far from being a cause for dejection, is meant to be a spur to progress.

Assuming that our hearts are set on pleasing the Lord, we can count on his love and acceptance as we come to the Lord's table. I don't write off my thirteen-year-old son just because he isn't as mature as my older son of twenty-three. Sure, he has a long way to go, but for a boy of thirteen he's just fine. That's how our Father views us — miles from maturity but working hard at it, emulating our 'Elder Brother' and a joy to have around.

Devotees of the worm mentality who are still unconvinced should now turn to their Bibles and read right through the New Testament. Having studied the evidence, let them decide whether they should approach the Lord's table as 'miserable sinners' or as children of the household, loved and accepted.

Recognising the body

What, then, *does* Paul mean by self-examination? What does it mean to eat and drink 'in an unworthy manner'?

Paul himself provides the answer. The person who eats and drinks unworthily, and thus 'eats and drinks judgment on himself', is the person 'who eats and drinks *without recognising the body of the Lord'* (1 Corinthians 11:29), or 'without discerning the body' (RSV).

And what does this mean? To begin with, it may well include a contemptuous familiarity with the bread which betokens his body, a sinful over-casualness about the death of Christ, who 'bore our sins *in his body* on the tree' (1 Peter 2:24), a failure to take account of the awesome cost by which we were redeemed from slavery and brought into the covenant community. But the main reference, without question, is to 'the body of the Lord' in its figurative sense — *'the church, his body'* (Ephesians 5:23).

The word 'body' occurs some fifty times in 1 Corinthians. In most cases it means the human body, but in and around the passage on the Lord's Supper in chapter 11, Paul uses it to describe the church, as he also does in his letter to the Ephesians. '*You* are the body of Christ,' he says to the Corinthians, 'and each one of you is a part of it' (1 Corinthians 12:27). Again, 'We were all baptised by one Spirit into one body' (1 Corinthians 12:13), and, 'Because there is one loaf, we, who are many, are one body, for we all partake of the one loaf' (1 Corinthians 10:17).

Therefore, as Barclay explains, when it comes to failure to recognise the body in our taking of the bread and wine, 'The person condemned is not the person who does not discern that the elements he takes in his hands are the Lord's body . . . but the person who does not discern that *Christians are the Lord's body, and must be in unity before they dare approach the sacrament.*'[2]

In other words, to eat and drink unworthily, to eat and drink judgment upon ourselves, is to come to the Lord's Supper when there is *something wrong in our relationship with our fellow-believers in the local church.*

We are 'guilty of sinning against the body . . . of the Lord' when we treat our fellows with shallow respect. And we are 'guilty of sinning against the . . . blood of the Lord' (1 Corinthians 11:27) when we '(treat) as an unholy thing the blood of the covenant' (Hebrews 10:29) by taking the covenant symbols while failing to bless our brothers with covenant courtesies.

It is failure in such matters as these that calls down the fatherly judgment of God upon us. And his is no token judgment, a mild slap on the wrist for the sake of appearances. At Corinth some were weak, some were ill and some had actually died.

God doesn't change; we are liable to similar penalties today if we indulge in similar vices. For our own instruction and safety, therefore, we must now look to see exactly what those vices are.

Chapter 16 NOTES

1. E.F. Kevan, *The Lord's Supper,* Evangelical Press, 1966, p27
2. W. Barclay, *The Lord's Supper,* SCM Press, 1967, p109. Italics mine

Sins against the body — 1

Division

Paul's major cause for complaint at Corinth was *division*.

Division destroys the unity of the church, and the maintenance of unity was an issue of deep concern to Paul. It is an issue of equal concern to Christians today, though many tackle it from the wrong end. They strive for Catholic-Anglican unity, for example, and Anglican-Methodist unity. They organise interdenominational consultations and ecumenical get-togethers. But on the premise that charity begins at home, Paul zeroes in on unity in the *local* church.

In his letter to the Corinthians, he jumps in with the unity question right at the beginning: 'I appeal to you, brothers, in the name of our Lord Jesus Christ, that all of you agree with one another so that there may be *no divisions among you* and that you may be perfectly united in mind and thought' (1 Corinthians 1:10). It comes up again later when he broaches the issue of the Lord's Supper (10:17; 11:17-22).

Party spirit

Unity is a covenant issue, and so is the Lord's Supper. It is because we are all children of the same Father that we belong to the one family, and the covenant meal is the expression of that oneness. Lack of unity at the Supper, therefore, is as much a contradiction as a kosher bacon sandwich. But something that calls down the judgment of God is no laughing matter.

The Corinthian church was split into factions attached to certain leaders (1:11-12). The pro-Paul party were probably the harkers back to the 'good old days'. Paul had been gone from Corinth for several years now, but their personal debt of gratitude for his efforts in bringing them to the Lord doubtless provoked comments like, 'I suppose our present leaders are OK, but for me there'll never be anybody to touch Paul.'

The pro-Apollos party were in all likelihood the intellectual élite. A tidy-minded lot, they admired Apollos's eloquence, the clarity of his teaching and his masterly grasp of the Old Testament. Their present-day counterparts have bookshelves stacked with Puritan works and love to debate predestination, supralapsarianism and the five points of Calvinism.

The pro-Peter party, by contrast, were probably the legalists. For them, the first-century equivalent of opposition to cinema-going, wine-drinking, wearing make-up or blue jeans and the eating of ice-cream on Sundays provided a framework of 'holy' living which they were determined to impose on the rest of the church — for its own good, of course.[1]

Factions of these and other kinds are still alive and kicking in local churches everywhere: look out for the 'we prefer the old hymnbook' party; the anti-arm-raising party; the 'keep the pews' party; the pro-King James Bible party; the 'preach the sovereignty of God and forget the rest' party; the 'let's all be lovey-dovey and not rock the boat' party; the 'health and wealth' party; the 'signs and wonders' party; the pro-charismatics and the anti-charismatics; the Calvinists and the Arminians; those who support Billy Graham and those who don't; lovers and haters of guitars, organs, public appeals to accept Christ, choir robes, speaking in tongues and post-tribulation premillennialism.

It is one thing to hold opinions on some of these topics. It is another thing altogether to turn them into party issues, making the propagation of them the mainspring of our existence, to the neglect of our common life in Christ.

For diehard members of such different 'parties' to share bread and wine is farcical. In their everyday attitudes they are working against each other while, at the Lord's Table, they eat the one loaf which proclaims their unity and drink the blood of the covenant which says, 'We are one.' It's a dangerous practice.

Spiritual individualism

At the heart of all division lies *individualism*. For all the spiritual-sounding claims of the party in Corinth who said, 'I follow Christ,' these people were probably the most troublesome of all. Despising the hero-worship of the others, they treated *all* human leadership with suspicion.

They are around today. 'Our only leader is Jesus,' they claim, and excuse their often weird or outrageous behaviour with the mouth-stopping retort, 'The Lord told me . . . .' Though professing a kind of attachment to the local church, their ties are loose. For the most part, they do their own thing, coming and going as they please, rootless and unaccountable.

In Corinth, individualism appeared as selfishness and greed, even at the Lord's Supper. 'When you come together, it is not the Lord's Supper you eat,' complains Paul, 'for as you eat, each of you goes ahead without waiting for anybody else. One remains hungry, another gets drunk' (1 Corinthians 11:20-21).

Had the prophet Haggai been around, he would have voiced God's complaint as he had done over five hundred years earlier: 'My house remains a ruin, while each of you is busy with his own house' (Haggai 1:9).

While drunkenness at the Lord's Supper would be unthinkable to most Christians today, an underlying individualism in the taking of the bread and wine often remains. In fact, the personalisation of the Lord's Supper is probably its number one problem area today. Christians take it as individuals, not as members of a covenant community. Many haven't the remotest idea that in it their Lord is crying, 'You belong to each other!'

Self-centred partaking has its roots in mediaeval Catholicism, where to eat the wafer was to eat Christ, and the more you consumed, the more grace you enjoyed and the more personal spiritual credit you accumulated. It took the Reformation to expose the folly of that approach. While Luther moved some way in the right direction, it was Zwingli who truly grasped the Supper's implications of covenant and unity.

Barclay writes: 'For Zwingli the sacrament was a demonstration of, and a way towards, the unity of those who are in the new covenant, and a pledge to live life according to that covenant obligation. "We eat this bread," he wrote to Alber, "that we may become one bread." '[2] He had seen something of vital importance.

Article XXVIII of the Church of England catches the right balance, too. It records that, first and foremost, 'the Supper of the Lord is . . . a sign of the love that Christians ought to have among themselves one to another'. What is needed, however, is for the covenant love and unity expressed in the Lord's Supper to rise up out of the pages of creeds and confessions and appear *in practice* in local churches today.

Twenty-five years ago I made a solemn vow to love my wife. I have a certificate to prove it. But what good is that if I fail to love her in practice today? God, who in his covenant love declares, 'Never will I leave you, never will I forsake you' (Hebrews 13:5), is longing for Christians, first of all in local churches but ultimately across the churches, to look one another in the eye and say the same words *to each other*.

That's what covenant love means. Only when we lay down our sinful individualism will it even begin to be possible.

Private communion?

It is appropriate here to mention the common practice of 'private communion' — the carrying of the bread and wine by a minister to an individual who, usually because of sickness or infirmity, cannot attend regular communion services.

The New Testament insists, however, that the Lord's Supper is a communal affair. Bearing in mind that 'communion' (Greek *koinonia*) means 'sharing', the two words 'private' and 'communion' are contradictory. How can one take privately what is essentially corporate? It is like a company director having a board meeting on his own.

If the church is what we *are*, the infirm church member, even though unable to travel to the usual meeting-place, is still part of the church. This means that fellow-believers will be in and out of the house all the time, bringing meals, cleaning and cooking, praying, shopping, singing and otherwise expressing their covenant commitment. The most natural way for the infirm one to enjoy the Lord's Supper which expresses that commitment is for a dozen of the saints, representative of the whole church, to descend on the house and share the bread and wine with him or her round the fire one evening.

In a hospital, three or four can usually gain permission to do something similar at a patient's bedside — a far cry from the lonely and ritualistic serving of the elements from a little black bag accompanied by a ramble through the set prayers.

If, in cases of severe illness, no more than two visitors at a time are allowed, let one of the elders and his wife visit and say, 'All the church would be here if they could, Mary, but obviously that's impossible. So we're here to represent them today, and we have bread and wine to share with you.'

Then, as *all three* eat and drink (for single participation is meaningless), let them say something like, 'Mary, this is a reminder that, because we each belong to Jesus, we also belong to each other. We're committed to you now as much as ever before, because the Lord himself has joined us. We'll never ditch you or forget you, so just relax and rest. We're going to pray now and ask God to bless you. In the meantime, be assured that we're keeping an eye on your house. Brian and Janice have got the cat, and we've just paid your gas bill for you.'

In that kind of context, the Lord's Supper is a feast of fellowship and love. After the visitors have left, Mary looks at the crumbs left on the bedcover and lifts her heart in worship to the Lord who sets the solitary in families (Psalm 68:6).

To summarise, then: the covenant meal is incompatible with both *division* and *individualism*. To try to combine it with either is to invite the judgment of the Lord. But there are other attitudes which are equally at odds with the Supper, and to these we now turn.

Chapter 17 NOTES

1. A helpful analysis of the various factions in Corinth can be found in D. Prior, *The Message of 1 Corinthians*, IVP, 1985, p29f
2. W. Barclay, *The Lord's Supper*, SCM Press, 1967, p77

Sins against the body — 2

Betrayal

Judas Iscariot will stand for ever as the personification of another sin against the covenant community — *betrayal.*

Betrayal is the brother of *hypocrisy,* and they usually travel together. Earlier, we highlighted the need for reality in our dealings with each other in the local church. Unless we fiercely maintain that reality, the twin brothers will take over.

Betrayal means putting on an air of friendliness and support while, inside, the heart is full of spite and malice. It is Judas greeting Jesus in the customary way with a chummy 'Rabbi!' and a kiss while, in the very act, he is setting him up for arrest (Mark 14:45-46). It is the smiling Baptist deacon shaking the pastor's hand on a Sunday morning with, 'Good morning, George, lovely to see you,' while in the background he is drumming up support to get George voted out of the pastorate at the next church meeting.

To take the Lord's Supper with a heart full of betrayal is, like Judas, to put one's head in the noose. Just to live in that hypocritical way is bad enough, but the heightening of reality which takes place at the covenant meal makes it an abomination. One of the worst curses that Obadiah could find to pronounce upon Edom was the betraying of a solemn trust founded on covenant. 'Your friends will deceive and overpower you,' he declared; *'those who eat your bread will set a trap for you*, but you will not detect it' (Obadiah 7).

'God deliver us from such a fate!' we may well respond. It hurts to be betrayed. But let's remember that our brothers and sisters in Christ are probably praying the same. By our total determination to be frank and righteous in all our dealings with them we can be part of the answer to their prayers.

Experience shows that church leaders are the ones most liable to be betrayed. Happy is the pastor or elder who is approachable enough for the people to express their misgivings, strong enough to lead them on what he believes to be the right course, and secure enough in their covenant commitment to lead from the front and, in so doing, turn to face the future without fearing a stab in the back.

Grumbling

He will be happy, too, if his church is free from *grumbling*, for this is another sin against the body which tends to focus on leaders. Grumbling figures prominently in John 6, where Jesus talks about eating his flesh and drinking his blood — as if to show how inappropriate it is in such a context (see John 6:41, 43, 61). 'Don't do it,' is Paul's advice to the Corinthians. Drawing illustrations from the history of Israel, he commands, 'Do not grumble, as some of them did' (1 Corinthians 10:10).

In the final analysis our grumbling, though directed at church leaders, is grumbling against God (1 Corinthians 10:9). It is putting the Lord's patience to the test by our impatience and constant griping. Again, it is a dangerous occupation. How, with impunity, can we break covenant bread with the leader we grumble about, in the presence of the very God of covenant who takes our grumbling personally?

Idolatry

To Christians in the Western world it may seem out of place to caution against *idolatry*. But when we consider Paul's identification of idolatry with greed (Colossians 3:5), it embraces us all.

Covenant means the opposite of greed: generosity. How can we take the bread and wine of covenant commitment when we shrink from sharing our cash, our time, our skills, our car with our covenant brothers? What kind of covenant love is it that turns up its nose at tithing and thinks it has done both God and the local church a favour when it puts no more than the price of a pint of beer into the offering?

For the Corinthians, of course, literal idols were on every hand. Many of the Christians there had been raised on idol worship and the heathen feasts that went with it. In fact, this is the context of Paul's teaching on the Lord's Supper: 'You cannot drink the cup of the Lord and the cup of demons too; you cannot have a part in both the Lord's table and the table of demons' (1 Corinthians 10:21).

Idolatry smacks of compromise. Doubtless many of the attitudes Paul condemns in the Corinthians' behaviour at the Lord's Supper were a carry-over from paganism. While they loved the worship and the prophesying that went on in the church, a bit of pagan-style drunken revelry was also nice from time to time. But the prophetic voice of Elijah always challenges compromise: 'How long will you waver between two opinions? If the Lord is God, follow him; but if Baal is God, follow him' (1 Kings 18:21).

Elijah-days are upon us again. Covenant requires singlemindedness. No Christian worth the name, for example, can eat at the table of the Lord and, at the same time, at the table of a church-substitute like Freemasonry.

The astounding fact is that the Lord's Supper itself can become for some an object of idolatrous worship. To some extent that was even true of the Corinthians, who saw it as some kind of fetish.

Summarising chapter ten of 1 Corinthians, Howard Marshall observes: 'Paul's main purpose in this chapter was to lay a foundation for his warning to so-called "strong" Christians against thinking that the Christian sacraments could protect them from falling under judgment because of their sin and that they could cheerfully participate in pagan sacrifices.'[1]

Pagan sacrifices apart, the Lord's Supper is little more than a fetish to those who view it as a religious work which serves somehow to surround them with a wall of protection against evil. It is the equivalent of wearing a crucifix around the neck as a lucky charm or crossing oneself when danger threatens — pure paganism.

To bring idolatrous attitudes to the Lord's Supper is bad. To make an idol out of the Supper itself is worse, for it turns the covenant meal into a pagan feast. Can we wonder at the judgment of God?

Immorality

Finally, we must identify a sin which in Corinth was closely linked with idol-worship: the sin of *immorality*.

'All other sins a man commits are outside his body, but he who sins sexually sins against his own body,' says Paul (1 Corinthians 6:18). To sin against one's physical body is to sin against the spiritual body, the church, of which the former is a part. Abuse of the one inevitably leads to abuse of the other, for both are the dwelling-place of God by his Spirit (1 Corinthians 6:19; Ephesians 2:19-22).

In my experience, Christians who fall into immorality are often the superspiritual types. These latter-day gnostics drive a wedge between the spiritual (in their view the truly important) and the physical (the earthy and unimportant). They can continue praying and prophesying while they look you in the eye and say of an immoral sexual liaison, 'The Lord led us into it.'

But the Lord assuredly didn't! True spirituality is supremely down-to-earth and touches the most physical and practical areas of our lives — how we treat our husbands, wives and children, the way we talk, how we spend our money and do our work. Paul speaks with the voice of true spirituality when he states, 'We should not commit sexual immorality, as some of (the Israelites) did' (1 Corinthians 10:8).

God is keen on bodies. Our ultimate destiny is not to be disembodied spirits but to enjoy the kind of glorified body that Jesus had after his resurrection (Philippians 3:20-21). In the meantime we aim to honour God with our present bodies (1 Corinthians 6:20) by offering them to him as living sacrifices (Romans 12:1), unpolluted by sexual immorality.

Sexual sin is an infringement of the marriage covenant (Malachi 2:14). It is also a sin against the covenant into which God by his grace has called us. How can we indulge in it and continue to meet around the Lord's Table, like the incestuous man in Corinth, and expect to get away with it?

Jeremiah took even the old covenant people to task on the issue: 'Will you steal and murder, *commit adultery* and perjury, burn incense to Baal and follow other gods you have not known, and then come and stand before me in this house, which bears my Name, and say "We are safe" — safe to do all these detestable things?' (Jeremiah 7:9-10). How much more is this true in the new covenant community, the church of Jesus Christ, and at the table which expresses that covenant.

We dare not come to the Lord's Supper while practising the 'sins against the body' which we have outlined in these two chapters: division, individualism, betrayal, grumbling, greed (idolatry) and immorality. To do so is to eat and drink unworthily, failing to recognise the Lord's body, and so to eat and drink judgment upon ourselves.

And the answer, of course, is not to stay away from the Lord's table, but to stay away from the sins! By his grace we may do so (1 Corinthians 10:13).

Chapter 18 NOTES

1. I.H. Marshall, *Last Supper and Lord's Supper,* Paternoster Press, 1980, p123

Curses
and blessings

'Curses and blessings' — that's a heavy chapter-title for a book on the eucharist. Some readers, who launched into the book expecting a quiet cruise through the subject, may now be wondering how we managed to get into such stormy waters. Have we drifted off course?

Not at all. Let's summarise. We have noted Paul's call to examine ourselves before partaking of the Lord's Supper. We have pinpointed the kind of eating and drinking which, by means of that examination, he wants us to avoid, namely, eating and drinking 'without recognising the body of the Lord'. And we have clarified what that means: failure to take proper account of our brothers and sisters in the local church and of our covenant obligations towards them.

We have also seen how those obligations, binding at the best of times, become exceptionally so at the Lord's Supper, which by its very nature proclaims our covenant oneness in Christ. There is a heightening of reality in the taking of bread and wine which brings both the curses and blessings of the covenant into sharper focus.

Every covenant, remember, has its curses and blessings. They are the 'small print', the detailed terms of the agreement which come into force when the 'document' is signed by the shedding of blood.

When Moses proclaimed the old covenant he made sure

the people understood that 'small print': 'See, I am setting
before you today a blessing and a curse — the blessing if you
obey the commands of the Lord . . . ; the curse if you disobey
the commands of the Lord' (Deuteronomy 11:26-28; see also
28:1-68). The new covenant, too, offers both penalties and
benefits, curses and blessings, brought into force by the
shedding of the 'blood of the new covenant' at Calvary.

And what are those curses and blessings? We will first
consider the curses, partly because the situation Paul
addressed in Corinth required him to stress them in
particular, and partly so that, having got them out of the way,
we can strike a happier note to finish with!

Sickness and death

The person who eats and drinks without recognising the body
'eats and drinks *judgment on himself'*, Paul explains, adding,
'That is why many among you are *weak and sick,* and a
number of you have *fallen asleep (in death)'* (1 Corinthians
11:29-30). The curses, then, are sickness and death.

Weakness and sickness in the Greek are similar to each
other in meaning and should be seen as one. As in the game
of soccer, they are the 'yellow card' of warning that we are
infringing the terms of the covenant. If we fail to heed that
warning, there is a 'red card' to follow, a literal 'sending off'
from this life's field of play. In other words, unless we deal
with the sin against the body which is causing the weakness
and sickness, they will soon result in death.

Presumably there is also an option of death without
previous sickness, as was the case (in a different context) with
Ananias and Sapphira (Acts 5:1-11).

We all have to die sooner or later, of course. But the death
Paul refers to is 'sooner' — it is *premature* death, death that,
given a right attitude to the covenant meal, could have been
postponed, perhaps for many years.

Premature death as a result of sin is well illustrated in
Scripture. Eli, the high priest of Israel in Samuel's youth,
received a reprimand for his lackadaisical attitude to a

different meal — the one he used to eat with his family as part of the Tabernacle service. A man of God pronounced a curse on him which has much in common with Paul's statement of eleven hundred years later: 'I will cut short your strength and the strength of your father's house, so that there will not be an old man in your family line . . . and all your descendants will die in the prime of life' (1 Samuel 2:31).

Shortly afterwards, Eli's sinful sons, Hophni and Phineas, both of them priests, fulfilled the curse when they died in battle (1 Samuel 2:34; 4:11).

Then, in the very section of 1 Corinthians where he deals with the Lord's Supper, Paul lists the many premature deaths which took place among the Israelites for some of the sins he warns us against today.

First, there is idolatry, and the attendant immorality: 'Do not be idolaters, as some of them were . . . . We should not commit sexual immorality, as some of them did — and in one day *twenty-three thousand of them died*' (1 Corinthians 10:7-8; see Exodus 32:1-6; Numbers 25:1-9). Next, there is the impatience that tests the patience of God: 'We should not test the Lord, as some of them did — and were *killed by snakes*' (1 Corinthians 10:9; see Numbers 21:4-9). Finally, there is grumbling: 'Do not grumble, as some of them did — and were *killed by the destroying angel*' (1 Corinthians 10:10; see Numbers 14:2-4, 26-30; 16:1-35).

As for betrayal, we have the grim example of Judas who, after his betrayal of Jesus for money, met a premature death — even if it was self-inflicted: 'he went away and *hanged himself*' (Matthew 27:5).

Jesus: an early death

But most significantly, *Jesus* died prematurely, 'cut off from the land of the living' in his prime, at the age of thirty-three (Isaiah 53:8). Like the thousands of Passover lambs before him — slain at only one year old — 'he was led like a lamb to the slaughter' to become *the* Passover lamb for us. In the greatest exchange of all time, he endured the covenant curse of premature death so that the covenant blessings of health and life could become ours.

Every time we partake of the Lord's Supper this truth is brought to mind. What an incentive to steer clear of the sins which spoiled the covenant community of old! If the God whose name is Jealous (Exodus 34:14) dealt severely with the community bought by the blood of ordinary lambs, how much more severely is he going to deal with the community bought 'with the precious blood of Christ' (1 Peter 1:19)?

God's judgment, when it does fall, is not for judgment's sake. He's not that kind of God. Paul is clear: 'When we are judged by the Lord, we are being *disciplined* so that we will not be condemned with the world' (1 Corinthians 11:32). His judgment is an expression of his personal care for us and his desire for the wholeness of the covenant community. He takes a firm line with his family *because* we are his family.

Not all sickness stems from personal sin, of course, but much of it does. Could some of our present ailments, perhaps, be attributed to anti-covenant attitudes towards our brothers and sisters in the local church, and especially at the covenant meal? If so, the answer, I must stress again, is not to skip the Lord's Supper — because the judgment of God also operates outside of it — but to correct the wrong attitudes, speak the truth in love and so line ourselves up, not for curses, but for blessings.

A means of grace

And are there, in fact, blessings to be found in eating worthily, just as there is judgment in eating unworthily? Or to put it in more theological terms, is the Lord's Supper a 'means of grace'?

Most certainly. If it can produce practical results of a painful nature it can also do the reverse. The blessings are as potent as the curses. But we must not be so naïve as to imagine that grace flows from the Lord's Supper in some mechanical sense, that we just turn up, eat the bread and drink the wine and — hey presto! — blessing comes out of the hat.

An ordinary meal, because it contains vitamins and other nutrients, strengthens simply by being eaten. It gives nourishment regardless of the attitude of the eater. But not so the Lord's Supper. Whether we draw from it benefit or pain depends entirely on the attitude in which we eat it. It is our recognising of the Lord's body — our covenant attitude to our brothers and sisters in Christ — which makes it a means of grace.

All too easily the Lord's Supper can become a 'ceremonial food', especially in ritualistic churches. But 'it is good for our hearts to be strengthened by *grace*, not by ceremonial foods, which are of no value to those who eat them' (Hebrews 13:9). The Supper, therefore, becomes a means of grace only to those who have already been 'strengthened by grace'. In other words, we receive grace *from* the Lord's Supper when we first bring grace *to* it.

This is exactly where the Corinthian Christians were going wrong. They came to the covenant meal living in the good of *saving* grace, no doubt, but they had failed to keep drawing upon God's *sustaining* grace. Our initial salvation is by *grace*, through *faith* (Ephesians 2:8). But grace doesn't end there; the Lord wants us to go on receiving from his fulness 'grace upon grace' (John 1:16 NASB). Neither does faith end there, for the righteousness of God is 'from faith to faith' (Romans 1:17 NASB). We reach out in constant faith to draw upon the supply of God's constant grace.

'See to it that no-one misses the grace of God,' warns the writer to the Hebrews (12:15), referring to sustaining rather than saving grace, and then goes on to list some of the sad consequences for those who do. These turn out to be some of the very sins by which Christians eat and drink judgment on themselves: bitterness (expressed in grumbling and betrayal), immorality and idolatrous materialism (12:15-16).

Grace through covenant love

And how, you may ask, do we exercise that grace-grasping

faith? James's answer is plain: by works, or deeds (James 2:14-26) — by what we *do*.

We may not be saved *by* good deeds, but we are certainly saved *for* them (Ephesians 2:8-10). So, prompted by both the Spirit and the Word, we set out actively and deliberately to do the will of God. Straightaway, we hear him say, 'Love your brothers and sisters with the same covenant love that I have shown to you' — not sloppy sentimentality but the robust, practical sharing and caring which the New Testament calls *agapé* love.

What is love? Love is baking an extra cake to give to Cynthia, who recently sprained her wrist. Love is using some of your annual bonus to pay for Fred and Alice to have a weekend away on their own, while you fix to look after their four young children. Love is sitting down and encouraging the boy who, in spite of hard work, didn't get the exam grades he'd hoped for. Love is lending out your car when someone in the church needs it more than you do.

Love is a phone call to say, 'I was really blessed by your prophecy in the meeting this morning.' Love is anonymously slipping £20 through someone's letterbox late at night in response to the prompting of the Spirit. Love is a warm hug accompanied by 'It's great to have you around.'

Faith expressed in *agapé* love (Galatians 5:6) plugs us into God's grace, which we then take with us to the Supper, only to find, to our delight, that it attracts more grace. The whole thing is the opposite of a vicious circle — a blessed circle!

And the grace we receive is no airy-fairy nonentity; it has a practical manifestation. Just as unworthy eating results in sickness and death, worthy eating results in *health and life*.

That was the case under the old covenant, and it continues under the new one. When the Israelites moved out of Egypt at the exodus, 'no-one faltered' (Psalm 105:37), or, as the Revised Authorised Version expresses it, there was 'none feeble' among them — in spite of years of abuse under their taskmasters. Covenant health and life were theirs at the start. And if they continued to live as a covenant people, God said,

'I will not bring on you any of the diseases I brought on the Egyptians, for I am the Lord, who heals you' (Exodus 15:26).

A better covenant — greater blessings

All this was under the old covenant. But the new covenant is 'superior to the old one' in every way (Hebrews 8:6)!

Some seem to think that the new covenant blessings of forgiveness and the gift of righteousness are so enormous that the relatively minor blessing of health has had to be forfeited to achieve it. That smacks of motor insurance politics. I recently took out a 'no claims bonus protection option', allowing me up to three claims in two years without losing my bonus. But there was a price to pay. In addition to the increased premium, I now had to pay an excess on each claim.

But God isn't like that. Far from sacrificing the physical benefits of health and healing to secure for us the spiritual blessing of sins forgiven, he has improved the benefits all round. At the cross, a more valuable 'blood of the covenant' was shed. Jesus, whose constant attention to the sick had declared God's concern for our physical health, 'took up our infirmities and carried our diseases' in an even deeper way when he died (Matthew 8:17).

Now, as a result, the beneficiaries of the new covenant can 'place their hands on sick people, and they will get well' (Mark 16:18).

More specifically, within the covenant community a sick person is invited to call for the elders to anoint him with oil and pray for him, 'and the prayer offered in faith will make the sick person well; the Lord will raise him up'. Then James adds some telling words: 'If he has sinned he will be forgiven. Therefore confess your sins to each other and pray for each other so that you may be healed' (James 5:14-16).

Isn't this the very kind of behaviour which we have seen to be appropriate to the covenant community, and which we should bring to the Lord's Supper? Frankness, concern, openness, mutual confession, caring, prayer for one another — they are blessings in themselves. But heightened by the intimacy of the covenant meal, they unleash a power for healing and wholeness beyond the ordinary.

Yes, there are blessings, as well as cursings, at the Lord's Supper. Health and life are there for all those who will approach it with the grace of obedience. Covenant love in the covenant community unlocks the fulness of covenant blessing — especially at the covenant meal.

Expectation and evangelism

The Lord's Supper has many facets, as we have seen. It is a look *back* to the cross and the roots of our salvation. It is a look *up* to where the living Christ is seated at God's right hand. It is a look *inside* in self-examination, and a look *around* at our covenant brothers. But it is also a look *forward*.

'Whenever you eat this bread and drink this cup,' says Paul, 'you proclaim the Lord's death *until he comes*' (1 Corinthians 11:26). We can't call ourselves New Testament Christians if the return of Jesus isn't at the forefront of our thinking.

The messianic banquet

I don't know how you picture the blessedness of that time when we will be united with our Lord for ever, but Scripture, in its delightfully earthy manner, expresses the great reunion in terms of a *meal:* 'Blessed is the man who will eat at the feast in the kingdom of God' (Luke 14:15).

Bearing in mind that a meal is a focus of all that is best in camaraderie, joy and satisfaction, the use of this figure is hardly surprising. It occurs again and again.

In Jesus' eschatological (end-time) parables, the five wise virgins accompany the bridegroom (Jesus himself) into the wedding banquet (Matthew 25:10); a great king prepares a wedding feast for his son only to find that the invited guests (the Jews) make excuses, so he fills the places with Gentile outsiders (Luke 14:16-24; Matthew 22:1-14); the master will treat his watchful servants to a meal at which he himself will serve them (Luke 12:35-38); 'people will come from east and west and north and south, and will take their places at the feast in the kingdom of God' (Luke 13:28-30). And as they sat at the Last Supper, Jesus promised his disciples that they would 'eat and drink at my table in my kingdom' (Luke 22:28-30).

The connection with the Lord's Supper is obvious. Indeed, it was at the institution of that supper that Jesus, after saying, 'This is my blood of the covenant, which is poured out for many for the forgiveness of sins,' went on to mention the great end-time feast: 'I tell you, I will not drink of this fruit of the vine from now on until that day when I drink it anew with you in my Father's kingdom' (Matthew 26:28-29).

He wasn't referring to the eating and drinking that he would do with his disciples between his resurrection and ascension (Acts 10:41). Not until his ascension did he take his throne and begin to reign (Ephesians 1:19-22; Philippians 2:9-11). At that point he set about that subduing of his enemies which will end only at his return. Then he will hand over the complete kingdom to his Father (1 Corinthians 15:24) and *the* feast can begin.

That messianic banquet, the great 'wedding supper of the Lamb' (Revelation 19:9), will be the feast to end all feasts. What a tremendous celebration it will be, as all the redeemed of the Lord, united once and for ever, feast their souls and bodies on the lavish bounty of the Lord while they feast their eyes on his beauty!

Overlap of the ages

But notice that it is the wedding supper of the *Lamb*. Even there, all the age-long associations of the Passover and the covenant blood will remain primary. And since we live in the overlap of the ages, living in this present age but having 'tasted . . . the powers of the coming age' (Hebrews 6:5), we have in the Lord's Supper a foretaste of that great supper to come, an occasion for the same gladness, fellowship and satisfaction, albeit on a smaller scale.

Can you imagine myriads of glorified believers sitting in the presence of their Lord in glory with their heads bowed, delicately sipping and chewing in stony silence? Certainly not! I can picture beaming faces, hugs and embraces, whoops of delight and sighs of deep satisfaction — covenant fellowship *par excellence.* I tell you, being drunk in the Holy Spirit (see Acts 2:15-21) will have nothing on the glorious spiritual intoxication we will know then, when the one upon whom the Spirit was poured out without measure will open his wine cellar to his brothers and sisters and throw away the key!

Then let our sharing of the Lord's Supper, which betokens the supper to come, be marked by something of the same holy informality. It speaks of our happy oneness in Christ's covenant fellowship, so let's express it. Let the fulfilment, joy, good companionship, love, trust and commitment of that coming feast be seen in our feasting here and now.

The Israelites ate the Passover ready for a journey. They had a future in mind as they ate it. We, too, eat the Lord's Supper with a future in mind, 'until he comes'. And if, in the meantime, we are called upon to share Jesus' cup of suffering as we live for him in a hostile world, let it serve to keep our eyes all the more on the glorious feast to come.

Something to proclaim

Between now and then we have a job to do. A weary world awaits the message of the gospel which it is our privilege to proclaim. In Greek, 'proclaim' is *katangello,* a word meaning to preach, to show or to declare, and it is this word that Paul uses in declaring, 'Whenever you eat this bread and drink this cup, you *proclaim* the Lord's death until he comes' (1 Corinthians 11:26).

What does he mean? He can't be suggesting, can he, that there is an evangelistic aspect to the Lord's Supper?

Marshall comments on this phrase that 'the bread and the cup point to the death of Jesus as a means of salvation, and thus proclaim to all who witness the Supper that Jesus died for them'.[1] He seems to be saying that the proclaiming is done to the believers who partake. But since, in its use elsewhere, *katangello* is used chiefly of proclaiming in an evangelistic sense (for example Acts 4:2; 13:5, 38; 17:3; 1 Corinthians 2:1; 9:14; Colossians 1:28), we have every reason to see the Lord's Supper as a means of preaching the gospel to unbelievers.

In what sense can this be so? *How* do we proclaim the Lord's atoning death? Certainly there is no intrinsic evangelistic power in the bare act of eating bread and drinking wine. But there is enormous evangelistic power in what that eating and drinking highlight: covenant love between Christians united in their love for Jesus.

Paul assumed that unbelievers would sometimes come into Christian gatherings where, in all likelihood, the breaking of bread would take place (1 Corinthians 14:24). And even where they didn't, the relative lack of privacy in Bible times (as in third world countries today) would make eavesdropping on the Lord's Supper fairly easy.

And what would they see and hear? A demonstration of such warmth and love in the Holy Spirit as would make their empty hearts ache for a taste. I have seen it happen.

Preaching by demonstration

In my own local church, the Lord's Supper is most often celebrated in families, housegroups and other small groups, but sometimes we celebrate it unitedly in the main Sunday gathering.

Many hundreds of believers are there. After a time of worship, most of the chairs are stacked to the sides of the hall. Supplies of bread and wine are placed at various points around the room, along the corridors and in smaller rooms, and we get started. Groups of half a dozen or so can be seen all over the building, their hands joined or their arms round each other's shoulders, praying for each other and blessing each other as they share the bread and wine. Words of knowledge are spoken, along with words of encouragement. The sick are prayed for, those going through hard times are loved and supported.

Then groups will break up and divide, to join up for more of the same in different combinations. In some groups there are tears of joy and fellowship. In others, spontaneous songs of worship to Jesus break out. It can go on for an hour or more. They are precious times.

I have seen unbelievers in such meetings. Usually, it is made clear at the beginning of the meeting that the Lord's Supper is for born-again believers only. Nevertheless, the Christians do their best to draw the outsiders into one of the groups and express a desire to pray with them or for them, though without their participating in the elements.

Two things strike the non-Christians. First, the (to them) incredible degree of warmth, honesty, love and caring evident among the believers. And, second, the fact that they are barred from this act of communion which is the focus of that very warmth, honesty, love and caring.

I have seen non-Christians simply break up in the situation, dissolving sometimes into deep sobs as the demonstration of *agapé* love exposes the coldness and poverty of their own Christless existence. Their tears and brokenness say, 'I've seen covenant love in operation; I like what I see and I want in.'

I have observed a couple of Christians take such a person to one side and, Bible in hand, lead him or her to Christ there and then.

'All men will know you are my disciples if you *love one another,*' said Jesus (John 13:34-35). Particularly to a modern generation cynical about politicians and preachers alike, whom they see as verbal tricksters offering promises without substance, covenant love *demonstrated* has an appeal unmatched by any amount of mere preaching. And that demonstration comes with double force in the heightened reality of the Lord's Supper.

The evangelistic aspect of covenant living, and of its meal

in particular, appeared in the Jerusalem church: 'Every day
. . . they broke bread in their homes and ate together with
glad and sincere hearts, praising God and enjoying the favour
of all the people. And the Lord added to their number daily
those who were being saved' (Acts 2:46-47).

The Lord's Supper was daily, the sharing of the *agapé* meal
was daily, the gladness and sincerity and praising were daily.
And the result? Unbelievers were favourably inclined and
the conversions, too, were daily!

We are living in days of restoration. God grant that we
may recapture the reality of living as true covenant
communities. Above all, may we find grace to kick over the
traces of historically-imposed ritualism and recapture the
warmth and vitality of the Lord's Supper, the wonderful
covenant meal.

Chapter 20 NOTES

1. I.H. Marshall, *Last Supper and Lord's Supper*, Paternoster
Press, 1980, p113

21

A
living reality

Theory and doctrine are fine — in their place. But in the
end it is people and the world of living experience that
matters. In this book we have set out certain doctrinal
principles concerning the Lord's Supper, but many of you
will have been touched chiefly by the description of an actual
covenant meal in the last chapter. Perhaps it made you long
for something deeper, in a way that mere theory never could.

In this final chapter, therefore, I want to outline some other
examples of covenant meals. They are all true incidents in
which I have been personally involved.

The housegroup

I had been leading a housegroup in the church for several
months, a mixed bag of some fifteen singles and marrieds
varying in age from fourteen to seventy.

Tonight we were going to break bread together. It was
February, the time of dark mornings and evenings and general
low spirits, and several of the group had recently been through
difficult circumstances. Encouragement was needed.

First, we worshipped the Lord together for a while, then
I called everyone to attention.

'We're going to encourage one another,' I announced.
'We'll start with Andrew here. Now, Andrew, I want you
to keep quiet. The rest of you, I want you to chip in and

say what good qualities you see in him — the things about
Andrew which you've come to appreciate. Then we'll go
round the circle and do the same with each one. We don't
want flattery or a line of flannel — that's not God's way —
just sincere and honest observations. Understand? Now,
who's going to start the ball rolling?'

'OK, I'll start,' said one. 'The thing I like about Andrew
is that he's always the same — he's consistent, whatever the
circumstances. Myself, I tend to be more up and down, so
I find him a real source of strength.'

'He's got a great sense of humour,' offers another.

'You always feel he's taking a genuine interest in you.'

'I love the way he explains Bible verses that have blessed
him. He's so clear. He doesn't waffle — you know what I
mean? — and he's enthusiastic with it.'

'Andrew's a very generous person.'

'Yes, he is, and caring, too. He's the sort of person you
could go to for help.'

It only took two or three minutes, but it left Andrew
beaming. Then we moved on round the circle. An hour later,
everybody was beaming! At that point, a bottle of home-made
wine and a bread roll were brought in from the kitchen and
placed on the coffee-table.

'Lord,' I prayed, 'you've been a witness to all that's been
said here tonight. Thank you for the frankness and openness
of your people. We're all greatly encouraged. Outside, people
usually pull each other to pieces, but here we are, building
each other up instead.

'Thank you that Jesus died for us to make it possible.
Thank you for making us part of the redeemed community.
Bless us now as we share this bread and wine, the reminder
that we belong to Christ and to each other. Amen.'

Soon, groups of two and three were sharing the bread and
wine all over the room, praying for each other, calling down
God's blessing on each other and adding to the words of
encouragement already spoken. It all came to a head when
someone started up the song:

We are bound to each other in love
By the word of the Father above.
Through the blood of his Son
We are merged into one.
We are bound to each other in love.[1]

'We're standing with you'

Pearl and Richard had been known to my wife and me for years. When they first married and couldn't get into their flat straightaway, they lived with us for a few weeks. In due course, they became the parents of two boys and were seen as solid, faithful members of the local church.

Richard's bank job, however, proved increasingly frustrating, and they came to feel that a change to something of a more general accounting job would be good for him. So they talked to the church elders and concluded that they could well combine a new job with a move to another town, where their Christian experience would be of great value in a smaller church.

Several visits to a church two hundred miles away convinced them that this should be their new location. Early attempts to find a job there drew a blank but, certain of their guidance, they moved house anyway and were warmly received into the church, Richard continuing to commute from his bank job to the new house each weekend.

When, three months later, there was still no new job and the commuting was becoming burdensome, they came to spend an evening with us. Doubts were setting in about the rightness of the move they had made and they were generally in low spirits. We talked and advised them, but there was obviously nothing practical we could do to help, short of continuing to pray that the Lord would solve the job problem.

'But I want you to know,' I said to them as they sat on our settee looking dejected, 'that our commitment to you, and our determination to stand with you in prayer to see this business through, is as strong as ever. So let's break bread together.'

My wife produced from the kitchen a glass of *Côtes du Rhône* and a leftover dinner roll. She sat with Pearl and I sat with Richard, the four of us squeezed on to the three-seater settee. We put our arms around them and hugged them as we took the bread and wine.

'Calvary binds us together,' I told them. 'We're one in the new covenant, and we'll stick with you to see this thing through to a satisfactory conclusion. Now, Lord, the four of us agree in our request. Richard needs a job urgently now, so please will you fix it for him. As far as we can see, he's done everything humanly possible. Lord, will you now do the divine bit, please?'

We all wept. The expression of covenant is an emotional affair — and none the worse for that! Pearl and Richard left our house that night with nothing changed circumstantially but heartened and fortified by the expression of covenant in the Lord's Supper.

We continued in prayer, and heard a month later that the much-needed job had become a reality.

Listening to God

It's great when the Holy Spirit elbows aside our plans and gives a church meeting an unexpected direction. Some five hundred of us were in the meeting on this occasion. There had been a particularly beautiful flow of worship, praise and prayer, and the presence of half a dozen bottles of wine and a pile of bread rolls on a table in the front corner served as a reminder that we were planning to have the Lord's Supper at some point.

Normally, we conduct the Supper in the way described in the last chapter. But on this occasion, as the worship continued, the Lord spoke to us in prophecy about the importance of having a listening ear to hear his voice. He reminded us that he was a speaking God and that, by the still, small voice of the Holy Spirit, he wished to speak into our hearts as individuals.

'We need to act on that word,' said the elder who was leading the worship. 'Because we are all the blood-bought children of God, we can all expect to hear him speak to us in our hearts.

'As you know, we were planning to break bread this morning, and we will go ahead, but in view of the prophetic word, we will do it differently from the usual way. We won't leave our seats. I'm going to ask the stewards to pass the bread and wine along the rows, and I want each of you to remember, as you partake, that Jesus, who died to make you God's child, is alive in you by his Spirit. Quietly express your personal gratitude to him, then listen for his voice.'

And that's what we did. We must have sat in near-silence for fifteen minutes, the only sound a low murmur as we whispered our love to Jesus and quietly awaited his response. It was a lovely time, focusing on the vertical rather than the horizontal aspects of the covenant. Yet in it all there was a strong sense that, while we waited on God as individuals, we were doing so as part of a body. My personal love for the Lord, strengthened at the Supper, would surely warm the whole church. His personal word to me would enable me better to serve my brothers and sisters.

Across the barriers

I was at a conference of charismatic leaders. All kinds of backgrounds were represented there, including Methodist, United Reformed, Roman Catholic, Church of England and Pentecostal, as well as the newer churches whose forte is provocation rather than infiltration — a determination to press on with God without any traditional denominational restrictions.

On the final morning we took communion together. It was a simple affair, with the minimum of formality. And to my delight, everyone took part, including the Roman Catholic delegation.

I have to confess that I have no faith whatever that God wants to renew the historic structures of Christendom. To me, they are so far removed from biblical Christianity that I see no option but to 'abandon ship' and start all over again with local churches built on a scriptural foundation — a movement with which I have personally aligned myself.

Sitting opposite me, however, was an Anglican vicar prominent in the renewal movement, convinced that there is real hope for the Church of England. We knew each other's position on such issues and had long since agreed to differ. In the end, I am accountable to God for obeying his word to me. I can never be accountable for the vicar. And vice versa.

As people began to move around the room to break bread with one another, I went across to him and offered him some bread. Then we drank wine together.

'Brother,' I said, 'ecclesiastically speaking, you and I have next to nothing in common.'

'That's right,' he smiled.

'But I want you to know,' I went on, 'that I recognise you as my brother in the Lord, saved by the same precious blood and filled with the same Holy Spirit. I believe you to be a man of integrity, doing what you are convinced God has given you to do, just as I am. So let's forget our differences of approach and just rejoice in the fact that we are children of the same Father and belong to the one family of God.'

We hugged one another and prayed for each other briefly, momentarily touching an area of oneness is Christ that transcended our differences.

In God's order, the 'unity of the Spirit' (Ephesians 4:3) precedes 'unity in the faith' (Ephesians 4:13) — relational oneness in Christ comes before oneness in doctrine and practice. I can't imagine how that man's 'church renewal' path could ever merge with my own 'restoration' path. But with God all things are possible and, in the meantime, the sharing of bread and wine had helped us keep things in perspective by reminding us that we are one in the one covenant.

May it do the same for you.

Chapter 21 NOTES

1. Eli Charira. Copyright © 1971 Scripture in Song. Administered in Europe by Thankyou Music, PO Box 75, Eastbourne BN23 6NW

Bibliography

W. Barclay, *The Lord's Supper,* SCM Press, 1967

D. Bridge & D. Phypers, *The Meal that Unites?* Hodder & Stoughton, 1981

P.T. Forsyth, *The Church and the Sacraments,* Longmans, Green & Co., 1917

F. Kevan, *The Lord's Supper,* Evangelical Press, 1966

D. B. Knox, *The Lord's Supper from Wycliffe to Cranmer,* Paternoster Press, 1983

I.H. Marshall, *Last Supper and Lord's Supper,* Paternoster Press, 1980

D. Prior, *The Message of 1 Corinthians,* IVP, 1985

Scripture index

Index

(In multiple references, figures in **bold type** indicate main reference)